fresh
GROUNDED
Faith

Jennifer Rothschild

HARVEST HOUSE PUBLISHERS

EUGENE, OREGON

Cover by Abris, Veneta, Oregon

Cover photos © Stockbyte Photography / Veer; Angel Rodriguez / iStockphoto

Back cover author photo © Randy Bacon, www.randybacon.com

Interior images © iStockphoto

FRESH GROUNDED FAITH
Copyright © 2008 by Jennifer Rothschild
Published by Harvest House Publishers
Eugene, Oregon 97402
www.harvesthousepublishers.com

Library of Congress Cataloging-in-Publication Data

Rothschild, Jennifer.
  Fresh grounded faith / Jennifer Rothschild.
    p. cm.
  ISBN 978-0-7369-2575-4 (pbk.)
  1. Christian women—Prayers and devotions. I. Title.
  BV4844.R68 2009
  242.'643—dc22

                                                                    2008034550

Printed in the United States of America

08 09 10 11 12 13 14 15 16 / DP-NI / 10 9 8 7 6 5 4 3 2 1

To my faithful WomensMinistry.NET
and Java with Jennifer readers…

I've enjoyed our weekly coffee breaks
together over the years.
You have enriched my life.
May your faith always be
fresh and grounded!

Introduction

WHY FRESH GROUNDED FAITH? That's simple. It's because stale won't do.

Stale doesn't work with coffee, it doesn't work with pastries, and it certainly doesn't work in our relationship with the living God.

So is it strange comparing the two—a cup of great java and daily time with your Creator and Savior? I don't think so, and here's why. God goes to great lengths and employs all sorts of metaphors and word pictures to help us understand who He is, what He's like, and what's so very big on His heart.

He says, "Come, buy wine and milk without money and without cost" (Isaiah 55:1).

He says, "Taste and see that the LORD is good" (Psalm 34:8).

He says, "Listen, listen to me, and eat what is good, and your soul will delight in the richest of fare" (Isaiah 55:2).

He says, "If anyone is thirsty, let him come to me and drink" (John 7:37).

So why not compare our day-by-day intake of life and wisdom and joy from the Lord to a daily consumption of a wonderful, warm, rich, fragrant, stimulating, flavorful coffee drink at our favorite coffee shop?

And that brings me back to stale versus fresh. The best coffee shops grind their beans daily, perhaps several times each day. And when that superheated water engages with the dark, rich, ground java—ah...the steaming fragrance reaches right around the block to draw you in. Compare that (just for a moment) to buying a cup of coffee early in the morning, leaving it on the counter in the kitchen, letting it assume room temperature, and then microwaving it that evening.

No, no, no. It just won't do, will it? Coffee needs to be fresh, fresh, fresh.

So does our walk with God.

The prophet Jeremiah reminds us that "his compassions never fail. They are new every morning" (Lamentations 3:22-23). New. Fresh made. Flown in direct from heaven. Specially prepared to your individual tastes and needs.

God made an even bigger object lesson of this point when His people had set out across the desert from Egypt en route to the promised land. He gave them manna, breakfast from heaven, every morning of their journey. It came with the morning dew, light as the flakiest croissant, sweet as clover honey, and completely nourishing. The people of Israel understood that they were to go out every morning, when the air was cool and the sun was still low in the sky, and gather whatever they required for their daily needs.

But no one was to keep any overnight (except on the night of the Sabbath). This wasn't the kind of provision you'd stick in your pantry or wrap in a napkin and carry in your purse for a couple of days. No, God insisted—with stern warnings—that His people eat the manna as it was newly made and trust Him for a day's supply every day.

Our God is the God of fresh things. Fresh strength when we're weak. Fresh courage when we're afraid. Fresh endurance when we're spent. Fresh wisdom when we're at our wit's end. And fresh mercy and forgiveness when we've failed Him, failed others, and failed ourselves and our highest ideals.

He wants to meet us in a fresh way each day...preferably when the day is new. And His leading in our lives will include new plans, insights just out of the wrapper, and never-used, never-thought-of-before ways to cope with our situations, tackle our problems, and reach for a better, more joyful life.

Stale doesn't cut it. Not in coffee. Not in life. Not with God.

Why, then, fresh-*grounded* faith? *Grounded* simply means rooted. Stable. Secure. God's Spirit will give us insights from God's Word that we can really trust and depend on regardless of what we face, regardless of what we may need to endure. The Bible is 100 percent reliable, and God's Holy Spirit will be a never-failing teacher to us if we come to Him with a humble heart and a willing spirit.

So why shouldn't our faith be fresh...and rich, and stimulating, and fragrant, and pleasurable? Why shouldn't it give us a lift and little more spring in our step? Why shouldn't we compare the Christian life to a satisfying, delicious coffee drink in the morning?

It works for me! Maybe it will work for you too as you open this book and take your first sip...

How to Enjoy This Book

WOULDN'T YOU LIKE YOUR FAITH TO BE as fresh and satisfying as your morning coffee? It can be if you take some time each day for a cup of fresh-grounded faith.

You could call this a nightstand book or a suitcase book—one you read before bed or bring on vacation. But I like to think of it as a coffee-break book! It's a refreshing blend of inspirational devotions.

It could be a morning wake-up or an evening decaf wind-down...or maybe a mid-afternoon pick-me-up.

For the next few months, you can flavor your day with a cup of inspiration (and a shot or two of insight) that will help you make it through the daily grind. And don't worry if you don't have much time. A cup of *Fresh Grounded Faith* won't take any longer to sip and savor than your regular cup of morning Joe.

Each offering is concise and casual, and it slides down pretty easy. But you never know. Start chasing some of the verses and concepts contained in these pages, and you might find yourself with a much, much deeper experience than you expected. And that's okay too!

So how can you get the most out of each "daily cup"? First you start with a fresh-grounded thought—a story-driven insight into Scripture and life brewed up just to teach and inspire you. Some days the blend is bold, other days, more mild and delicate, but it's always rich and satisfying.

After you drink in the daily thought, it's your turn to consider what you've experienced and write down your thoughts in a section called What's Percolating in Me: My Response. I encourage you to jot down your response to the truth you just read. Do you identify? Do you agree? Does it make sense to you? Have you had a corresponding experience that taught you something similar? What did God show you about that fresh-grounded thought?

After you write down what's percolating in you, you get to tell God about it in Spill the Beans: My Prayer. This is the place to confess your fears, sin, concerns, or anything else you need to acknowledge to your heavenly Father.

Your daily cup ends with a section called Thanks a Latte! My Praise. Here you express your gratitude to the Lord for what He's teaching you, how He's leading you, and what He is doing in your life. This is the place for you to note praises and thanksgiving for what you've experienced during your time with Him.

Just as you swallow your last sip of coffee, your reading and journaling is complete! You're ready to take on the day, filled to the brim with all you need to remain grounded and fresh in your faith. So, my friend, grab your favorite mug and fill it with your favorite brew. If you want to add your Bible to the blend, so much the better! Get a pen, settle into a comfy chair, and enjoy—each daily cup is good till you drop!

JJR

fresh GROUNDED Faith

1

Beautiful Julie

AT A WOMEN'S CONFERENCE IN HOUSTON, I met someone truly beautiful. It was the first time in recent memory that I wished I possessed someone else's appearance.

She stood in line with the other women attending the Women of Faith conference, where I was signing copies of my new book. I knew something was special about her when she arrived because my husband patted my back as he read her name tag to me. Since I am blind, his silent pat spoke volumes to me. But before I could begin to understand what was being communicated in the quiet gesture, the woman standing in front of me introduced Julie.

"Jennifer," she said, "this is Julie; she is from Pakistan. She is only here for a few more weeks while she recovers from her burns." In broken English, Julie's sweet voice interrupted, "A man threw acid on me."

The incident occurred in a township in Faisalabad, where Julie worked as a telephone operator to help support her family. Some visitors to the public phone office used insulting words as they tried to persuade her to embrace Islam. They told her, "Beautiful girls like you should not remain in Christianity."

When one man tried to touch her inappropriately, Julie slapped him. He returned the next day and threw sulfuric acid directly on her face, burning and blinding her. Speaking from her hospital bed, Julie told an attending missionary, "If I survive, I will serve [the] Lord Jesus for the rest of my life."

A holy hush fell upon the women in the signing line as we all were riveted by her words. I could hear sniffles and quiet sobs. My eyes welled with tears. I could not speak as I made my way from behind the signing table to her. I was overcome with emotion as I bent down to hug this little giant of our faith.

Only 19 years old, Julie possessed a maturity most live a lifetime to achieve. By now, the line had formed a circle around our beautiful sister. She confidently announced that she was going home soon. I think that every woman gathered there felt exactly what I did at that moment.

"Home? Will you be safe?"

"No matter," she shrugged. "If something happens, I will be home with Jesus."

At this point, through my tears, I began to pray for her. What else can we do in our human frailty? I wanted to clutch her in my arms, run for the arena exit, put her in an airplane, and bring her home to Springfield, Missouri, to live with me. I have no doubt that I wasn't the only woman standing there that day formulating a plan for Julie's protection. Every woman with me was fighting back her maternal instinct to shelter Julie.

We all prayed. Women from all over Texas, strangers yet sisters, bowed our heads, wept, and petitioned our Father to protect our petite, brave, beautiful Julie as she returned to Pakistan.

As she walked away, Phil whispered a tearful phrase in my ear. "Jennifer, I wish you could have seen her. She's so scarred but so radiant."

I wanted to get up from my signing table where women had

gathered for my autograph and give Julie my seat instead. She was a hero. I wanted to learn from her about faith. I wanted her autograph. I longed for her beauty.

Julie's beauty comes from the radiance of Christ that is best revealed through our scars. It's a compelling strength that becomes realized only in our weakness. It's a beauty forged in the refining fire of trials, and a loveliness fashioned on the anvil of faithfulness.

I am sure you will have the privilege of meeting Julie someday. I'll bet she will have a signing table in heaven. If you don't recognize her when you get there, just look for me. I'll be in line, gratefully praising our Father God, who gave Julie courage, sheltered her, and brought her home.

But if you don't recognize me, then look to the front of the line. You will recognize Jesus. He will be the truly beautiful one, so scarred yet so radiant.

He will be standing for Julie just as He stood for Stephen so many years ago. Your eyes will well up with tears as you observe Julie's eyes meet His. I'm sure she'll get up from behind the table, humbly bow, and give Jesus her seat instead. For He is the hero. He is the author of our faith.

And it is His autograph, His name, we most want written upon our hearts.

And I heard every creature in heaven and on earth and under the earth and in the sea, and all that is in them, saying, "To him who sits on the throne and to the Lamb be blessing and honor and glory and might forever and ever" (Revelation 5:13 ESV).

What's Percolating in Me: My Response

_____

_____

_____

_____

Spill the Beans: My Prayer

_____

_____

_____

_____

Thanks a Latte! My Praise

_____

_____

_____

_____

2

Simple Message, Powerful Cross

As soon as I made it to the back of the plane, I plopped down into the middle seat, letting my cane rest in front of me. I bent to stuff my carry-on under the seat, and as I straightened up, I quickly folded my cane and placed it in the seat pocket.

No sooner had I buckled my seat belt than my cell phone chirped.

"Hi, honey," I responded. "Yes, I'm on the plane."

I was headed to a women's conference in Las Vegas. Phil updated me on the boys' day and then asked a few questions about some ministry details.

We ended the call, and as I stowed my phone, a voice next to me said, "Are you a Christian?"

"Yes," I said, "are you?"

The woman seated between me and the window muttered something about growing up Catholic and attending Bible studies sometimes, but she didn't answer yes.

I introduced myself to her and asked what her name was. She told me it was Cassie. Then there was an awkward pause. I smiled and looked forward, just assuming we were fumbling through the social awkwardness of not knowing what to say next.

Well, Cassie didn't feel awkward. She knew exactly what to say next. "Jennifer," she blurted, "If you're such a——Christian, why won't you shake my——hand?"

I was stunned beyond words. Cassie may have sat two inches away from me, but a huge invisible world obviously separated us. It took me a minute to figure out what had provoked her. In my moment of bewildered silence, she repeated herself even more loudly. "If you're such a——Christian, why won't you shake my——hand!"

By this time folks around us were quiet because she was so loud. I felt trapped and confused. Then it hit me—she must have extended her hand, and I, of course, hadn't seen it. She must not have seen my cane when I first sat down next to her. I didn't look like a blind person to her.

"Cassie," I said very calmly, "you may not have noticed when I walked up that I carried a cane. I'm blind. I'm guessing you reached out to shake my hand, and I didn't realize it. I would be happy to touch you. I would never refuse to shake your hand…"

Cassie burst into tears and began to tell me how sensitive she was because she's been so hurt in life. That opened up a torrent of emotions as my seat mate poured out her sadness and rejection in a flood of tears. As I grasped her hands, I began to smell the tequila on her breath and hear the emptiness in her voice.

Tipsy, sad, and terrified of flying, she now clung to me physically and emotionally. As the plane taxied and finally took off, she shook and whimpered like a scared child. I calmly whispered and reminded her about the peace, rest, and safety in the arms of God.

Once we reached 33,000 feet, the flight attendant interrupted Cassie's chaotic chatter with the usual announcement. "We've reached our cruising altitude. You may now use approved electronic devices and move about the cabin. We do recommend that while you are seated, however, you keep your seat belt fastened."

Oh, I knew I was staying put. Cassie had fastened both her arms and her fragile feelings to the blankety-blank Christian who wouldn't shake her blankety-blank hand.

The flight lasted an hour and 40 minutes, and for each of those 100 minutes I was breathing in tequila and praying for wisdom. Cassie poured out a sad story of her broken past, her search for God, and her guiding philosophies—a funky hybrid of AA, Dr. Phil, and the Dalai Lama. Every question she asked me, I answered.

When she asked a big theological question, I gave a big theological answer. She'd listen, reach into her bag for another little bottle, and drink in both the alcohol and the answers.

Frankly, my answers didn't seem to satisfy her nearly as much as the alcohol. I could tell I wasn't connecting. The Holy Spirit though, had been guiding me—I knew it. I could sense His presence. So why wasn't I getting through?

As quickly as I asked myself the question, I heard the Spirit answer, *Jennifer, simplify. Simplify!* From that point on, regardless of how complex her questions were, I answered simply, "God loves you...Jesus died for you." That about summed it up. And even as her head got cloudier, she seemed to understand more clearly.

My earlier pontification may have mildly amused a seminary

professor, but it was powerless to touch Cassie. Only when I stripped the message down to the profound simplicity of the cross did a bridge begin to form between our very different worlds.

As we parted ways, she raved about how she knew God had sent me to her. As I gathered my things, I repeated, "Don't ever forget, Jesus loves you. That's why He came. That's why He died. He loves you."

That's how it ended, simple and strong. I have no idea what happened to my broken, inebriated traveling buddy. I hope I will meet her in heaven someday and hear the whole story.

I can't be sure what happened in Cassie's heart as a result of that flight, but I know what happened in mine. I was in awe of the healing, calming power that exists only in the simple message of the cross. "God loves you. Jesus died for you."

All of those earlier words I had poured out to Cassie may have revealed my knowledge, but somehow (and I'm being brutally honest here) they had slowly stripped the cross of its power. I shrouded the clarity of the cross with amateur theological analysis. The truth is, that desperate, frightened woman on my flight didn't need a lesson in systematic theology to come to Christ.

Cassie didn't need my answers, she needed The Answer.

Everyone needs what you and I desperately need—the power that comes from the unadorned message of the cross. It is the power to be saved, and it is also the power to be satisfied in this life.

May you and I never complicate, cover, or cease to marvel at the simple message of the cross, for it is "the power of God at work, saving everyone who believes" (Romans 1:16 NLT).

You'll remember, friends, that when I first came to you to let you in on God's master stroke, I didn't try to impress you with polished speeches and the latest philosophy. I deliberately kept it plain and simple: first Jesus and who he is; then Jesus and what he did—Jesus crucified.

I was unsure of how to go about this, and felt totally inadequate—I was scared to death, if you want the truth of it—and so nothing I said could have impressed you or anyone else. But the Message came through anyway. God's Spirit and God's power did it, which made it clear that your life of faith is a response to God's power, not to some fancy mental or emotional footwork by me or anyone else (1 Corinthians 2:1-5 MSG).

What's Percolating in Me: My Response

_____

_____

_____

_____

Spill the Beans: My Prayer

_____

_____

_____

_____

Thanks a Latte! My Praise

_____

_____

_____

_____

3

Follow Your Heart

On August 28, 1963, Martin Luther King spoke to a quarter of a million listeners at the March on Washington. The message he spoke that memorable day has become one of the most important and well-known speeches in our nation's history.

But it almost didn't happen.

I learned recently that the speech Dr. King had placed on the podium didn't even include the words "I have a dream."

Yes, he had spoken often about that dream of his. He had written about, shared, and promoted his dream. Communicating that dream was his passion. But evidently, the night before such an important speech, his handlers became concerned that the dream phrase had been overused and would lose its impact.

So King and his closest advisors worked to develop a fresher message—one that wouldn't risk tired familiarity.

The result? A speech entitled "Normalcy—Never Again."

Dr. King took the stage and began to deliver his new message. As the story goes, the great civil rights leader was close to ending his nine-minute delivery when he stopped following his transcript and began to follow his heart. The result?

"I have a dream…"

Oh, what we would have missed if he hadn't followed his

heart that day! It would have been like pulling a beautiful golden thread right out of our national tapestry.

And now, here's a much less historical and not so consequential story.

I was asked to sing at Focus on the Family's chapel service several years ago. Beth Moore would be speaking. For many months leading to that chapel service, I had been singing my own arrangement of "It Is Well with My Soul." It was nontraditional and fit my range, style, and comfort level perfectly.

When I sang my arrangement, I was at my personal best. I was acting out of my passion. I hadn't even sung the original melody of that song in almost a year.

Before chapel began, the crowd gathered, and Dr. and Mrs. Dobson came into the auditorium. The lady in charge mentioned that "It Is Well" was one of Doc's favorite songs, and she was so happy I was singing it.

Well, that's all it took. The lady may have been trying to encourage me with that remark, but the actual effect was to unleash a queasy wave of fear and self-doubt that swept over me. Should I shelve my special arrangement and do the traditional version instead? Phil even asked me if that's what I was planning to do…suggesting that the familiar version would be what Dr. Dobson and the crowd would be expecting.

A new transcript lay before me.

I felt such pressure to follow it. But my gut was telling me to follow my heart, not the transcript of others' opinions.

Still torn as to what to do, I took the stage and sat at the piano before the great psychologist, his wife, and 2500 occupied seats. And then I began to play what I assumed everyone wanted me to play.

I sang the original rendition of the song, and to be honest, it wasn't my finest moment. As a matter of fact, I'm not even sure it was good. Afterward Phil asked me, "What happened?" That's always a big clue that it wasn't my most scintillating performance.

I should have followed in Dr. King's footsteps. I should have abandoned pressure and followed my passion. There comes a time in each of our lives when we have to follow our hearts—even if it's not the prescribed transcript that lays before us.

"I have a dream" was true Martin Luther King—it was his passion, and that is why it was, is, and forever will be compelling and effective.

The same applies to me and you. Sometimes we must risk following our hearts rather than the consensus. Sometimes we have to go with our gut rather than the measured opinions of others—even if they are professional and experienced.

The only one who can effectively share your gifts is you. When we are truly ourselves, following the convictions and gifting God placed within us, we will be effective.

When God's Spirit lives in us, we can trust His still, small voice that whispers while the majority yells. When we listen to His voice inside us, we can trust the promptings of our own hearts. To go against the respected views of others requires courage, but after my Focus on the Family debacle, I've made up my mind that's what I want to do from now on. I want to have the courage to lay aside the transcript sometimes and follow the voice inside.

It has taken decades for this crowd-pleasing gal to risk following my passion, to be the me God created rather than squeezing into the expected mold I think others anticipate.

"Normalcy—Never Again" or "I Have a Dream."
Need I say more?

> *Don't let the world around you squeeze you into its*
> *own mould, but let God re-mould your minds from*
> *within, so that you may prove in practice that the*
> *plan of God for you is good, meets all his demands*
> *and moves towards the goal of true maturity*
> *(Romans 12:2 PHILLIPS).*

❧

What's Percolating in Me: My Response

_____

_____

Spill the Beans: My Prayer

_____

_____

Thanks a Latte! My Praise

_____

_____

4

Petals

AN ANTIQUE MASON JAR TUCKED AWAY in my jewelry chest contains some of my most precious possessions.

To a casual observer, it may appear that the jar is full of mismatched potpourri. But in reality, each dried flower petal has been placed in the jar quite intentionally over the past 20 years.

Within the antique blue glass are the petals from the first roses that Phil gave me on Valentine's day when we were dating. Mixed in with these are rose petals from my bridal bouquet, from the roses he gave me on our first wedding anniversary, and from the dozen roses that proudly graced the hospital room after the birth of our first son.

Over the years, more petals have been added. If you look through the hazy glass, you can see miniature buds that once adorned the corsage I wore on Mother's Day after our second son was born. The tiny blossom reminders of my grandmother's funeral are scattered within the potpourri, along with faded blossoms from roses that my sons presented to me at one of my speaking events.

Though each rose petal is different in color, texture, and size, what they all have in common is that they once complemented beautiful roses, and each represents something very dear to me.

There is another Rose, a precious Rose, that is not contained in my old Mason jar. It is a Rose that first sprang up in ancient Bethlehem. It blossomed in a humble manger, in the garden of poor, ordinary, faithful parents, beneath the pure light of a bright star.

The beauty of the Rose was first beheld by some humble shepherds and later adored by some very wise men. Both humble and high were granted access to the Rose. In the Song of Solomon, many pious Bible students through the years have seen the beauty of Jesus in the one who calls himself the Rose of Sharon. What a lovely way to communicate who He is to each of us.

The picture of a rose shows Christ's beauty, and it also shows His desirability and accessibility to each of us. The rose is the chief of flowers for its beauty and fragrance, and our Jesus is the preeminent object of our desire. The sweetness of His fragrant life and words adds beauty to our dull and colorless world.

For Christ to be the Rose of Sharon shows that He is the Rose for all. Sharon was the ancient place where roses grew in fields, plenty and lovely. Jesus was not a rose that sprung up in a greenhouse, reserved for the rich or elite. No, He blossomed in a humble manger, where all could see, touch, and receive Him. His gospel is for all—rich, poor, old, young, seeker, and skeptic.

The Rose of Sharon yields a transcendent perfume that calls us to breathe in His beauty. If you come to the manger to see the Rose, you will notice that it is moistened with dew—the tears of mourning that remind us that He was the Rose destined to wear thorns and to shed the beauty of His scarlet petals for you and for me.

He did, my friend. You are the reason He brought His beauty to this earth. You are the reason; it was for your sin the beautiful Rose was crushed.

You are the reason the Rose arose.

Don't hide the beauty of the Rose of Sharon in a treasure box with all your other sweet memories or keepsakes. Wear the Rose upon your heart, upon your life. So many cynical, despairing people in our unhappy world need to catch the scent of His fragrance and be drawn into His garden.

> *For you know that it was not with perishable things such as silver or gold that you were redeemed from the empty way of life handed down to you from your forefathers, but with the precious blood of Christ, a lamb without blemish or defect. He was chosen before the creation of the world, but was revealed in these last times for your sake. Through him you believe in God, who raised him from the dead and glorified him, and so your faith and hope are in God (1 Peter 1:18-21).*

What's Percolating in Me: My Response

_____

_____

_____

Spill the Beans: My Prayer

_____

_____

_____

_____

Thanks a Latte! My Praise

_____

_____

_____

_____

5

Believing Is Seeing

MY HUSBAND AND I SAT OUTSIDE our favorite coffee shop, and Phil pulled out our local paper. His eyes landed on a story that captivated him, and he began reading aloud.

It was about a young woman named Minda. She was born in India 18 years ago without arms or legs. After learning about her physical deformities, her soon-to-be mom began to secure her adoption. It took longer than she hoped because Minda could not provide a fingerprint for her legal papers or passport.

As Phil read, we both became choked up with emotion. Minda is a budding artist. She cradles a brush between her chin and shoulder and paints with such talent that her art is worthy of her own show.

Though her artistry is impressive, what really inspired me was the list her adoptive mom found in her backpack when she was in the fourth grade. It contained 127 things she would do if she had arms or legs. Things like set her own alarm clock, make the sign of the cross, walk where there aren't sidewalks, jump with joy and clap her hands, and be tall.

The news reporter ended the article by disclosing Minda's purpose in life. Minda said her purpose is to show that God is good all the time, even when it doesn't look like it.

Minda is guided by the unseen. Even in a wheelchair, this courageous daughter of God walks by faith and not by sight.

Faith is a journey, a bumpy road at times where we embrace what we can't understand and believe what we can't see. In George MacDonald's tale *The Princess and the Goblin*, faith is portrayed as following an invisible thread.

After Princess Irene rescued Curdie from the goblins' cave by following her grandmother's thread, she pled with her companion to see what guided them.

"There. Don't you see it shining on before us?"

"I don't see anything," persisted Curdie.

"Then you must believe without seeing," said the princess; "for you can't deny it has brought us out of the mountain."

Just like the skeptical character in MacDonald's fairy tale, most of the time we don't see either. God's ways seem obscure to us. Yet we follow and trust and recognize that He has "brought us out of the mountain" of our hopelessness, darkness, and despair. To follow and trust even when we can't trace His path is to believe without seeing, allowing ourselves to be guided and governed by revelation rather than mere reason alone.

As MacDonald put it, "Seeing is not believing—it is only seeing. The real triumph of this life is to understand that 'believing is seeing.'"

Like precious Minda, when we trust God to act with goodness, we see His goodness. When we believe God to be faithful, we see His faithfulness. When we are convinced that God is love, we see His love everywhere.

The walk of faith requires following even when we can't see or understand. Zora Neal Hurston said, "Faith ain't got no eyes, but she's long legged."

It's true. One step at a time, we trust God more than we trust our feelings. One step at a time, we receive what we can't reckon. One step at a time, we accept what we can't avoid.

Do you know what has helped me follow this invisible thread?

Blindness.

It's true. As I believe Him to provide and guide, I see His leadership and provision. As I trust Him to comfort and teach me, I feel His hand and hear His voice. I think Minda has followed the same thread and has been led out of a mountain of sorrow and gloom.

When Thomas finally touched his Lord's nail-scarred hands, Jesus said to him, "Because you have seen Me, you have believed; blessed are those who have not seen, and yet have believed" (John 20:29).

Peter, perhaps remembering that remark, wrote these words years later:

> Though you have not seen him, you love him;
> and even though you do not see him now, you
> believe in him and are filled with an
> inexpressible and glorious joy (1 Peter 1:8).

I want that blessing—to see because I believe. Don't you?

Trust Him more today than you did yesterday. If you can't understand, just keep following. Though it may be dark right now, you will see that eventually He has led you out of the mountain.

As George MacDonald wrote, "Let us step into the darkness and reach out for the hand of God. The path of faith and darkness is so much safer than the one we would choose by sight."

*So we're not giving up. How could we! Even though
on the outside it often looks like things are falling
apart on us, on the inside, where God is making new
life, not a day goes by without his unfolding grace.
These hard times are small potatoes compared to the
coming good times, the lavish celebration prepared
for us. There's far more here than meets the eye. The
things we see now are here today, gone tomorrow.
But the things we can't see now will last forever
(2 Corinthians 4:16–18 MSG).*

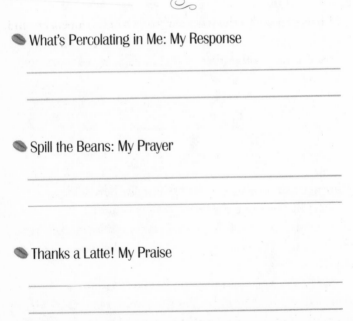

🫘 What's Percolating in Me: My Response

_____

_____

🫘 Spill the Beans: My Prayer

_____

_____

🫘 Thanks a Latte! My Praise

_____

_____

6

My First Stone

"I GOT MY FIRST STONE."

That was my big announcement at a luncheon with some of my favorite women. Patty has a gathering of her older friends at her home to celebrate various occasions, and this time it was Billie's birthday.

I happened to be the youngest woman at the luncheon, and I love listening to and learning from these seasoned and sage ladies. We discussed spiritual things, home décor, and of course, their grandchildren.

Then came the moment for my big contribution to the conversation: "I got my first stone."

There was an awkward pause.

I couldn't figure out why they were so shy to respond. *Maybe they're unfamiliar with stones,* I thought, *and how much better they are than traditional baking sheets. Or maybe they don't know how much better a pizza crust turns out on a stone.*

But my thoughts were interrupted by a brave older woman as she asked, "Honey, what kind of stone do you mean? Kidney or gall?"

I began to giggle. "I meant the kind you *bake* with!" They all chuckled and reminded me that the stones that come to mind during their stage of life have little to do with baking. Yet these gals knew their stuff and quickly began to tutor me on the proper use of stones.

"Don't use soap," one instructed.

"Oh—and if it breaks in your oven? The sound is awful, but don't be alarmed," another advised.

Since I left that luncheon, I have never used or thought of my stone in the same way. But here's what I have thought. *Thank You, Lord, for women who walk together, talk together, do life together, cry together, grow together, and laugh together.*

As Marcel Proust put it, "Let us be grateful to people who make us happy. They are the charming gardeners who make our souls blossom."

Does someone in your life make your soul blossom? Scripture reminds us that "oil and perfume make the heart glad, so a man's counsel is sweet to his friend" (Proverbs 27:9 NASB).

Your faith will continue to grow as you rub shoulders with faithful friends who give good counsel. Whether they instruct you about baking stones or lead you to the "rock that is higher" (Psalm 61:2), they will enrich your life. And if you don't feel you have that kind of friend, *become* one.

> *Keep me safe, O God,*
> *I've run for dear life to you.*
> *I say to GOD, "Be my Lord!"*
> *Without you, nothing makes sense.*
> *And these God-chosen lives all around—*
> *what splendid friends they make!*
>
> *(Psalm 16:1-3 MSG)*

🫘 **What's Percolating in Me: My Response**

_____

_____

_____

_____

🫘 **Spill the Beans: My Prayer**

_____

_____

_____

_____

🫘 **Thanks a Latte! My Praise**

_____

_____

_____

_____

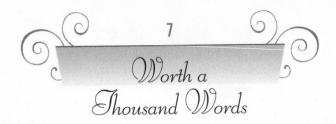

7

Worth a Thousand Words

SOMETIMES I LIKE TO READ THE GOSPELS as if I'm thumbing through a photo album chock-full of snapshots, glancing at each one. Recently, in Matthew 9, a great snapshot of Jesus reclining at a dinner party caught my eye.

It's a picture of Jesus and His disciples sharing a meal at Matthew's house—along with an apparently motley crew of sinners. The Pharisees in attendance that day with them were irritated and befuddled by how someone who claimed to be a rabbi could lower himself and have dinner with such riffraff.

The smug Pharisees asked Jesus' disciples about it. (And can't you just hear the contemptuous sniff?) "Why does your teacher eat with tax collectors and 'sinners'?"

Before His disciples could formulate their thoughts and answer the Pharisees, Jesus Himself spoke up. "It is not the healthy who need a doctor, but the sick" (Matthew 9:12).

Did you catch that? The Word specifically says that Jesus answered the question of the Pharisees even though it was asked of the disciples.

Now, why did Jesus answer a question that was clearly not directed to Him? The query was obviously aimed at Peter, John, and the boys. Maybe it's because the question directly related to Jesus and not to His followers.

Think about that for a moment. Keep your eye on that picture of Jesus and His disciples. Do you think the disciples gathered at Matthew's home that day could have answered the question well? If you were there, could you have answered well? Most likely they could have. And most likely you too could have come up with a reasonable defense for why Jesus chose to dine with society's lesser lights. But neither we nor His disciples could have answered as well as Jesus did!

This shows me that some questions are better left for Christ Himself, even if the questioner happens to direct the query at you or me. So here's a novel way of looking at it: Perhaps the questions that most directly relate to Christ should be left for Christ to answer for Himself.

People will ask questions like "Why do the innocent suffer?" Or maybe "Why does God allow evil?" The fact is, I really don't have a lot of zingy answers when I am confronted with those kinds of questions. As His disciple, I have an idea, but I don't hold the definitive answers. Only God does.

To assume ownership of the mysteries of God, as if I truly understand and can explain them, would be an arrogant, ignorant thing to do, and it wouldn't help the honest questioner at all. On the other hand, to pause after a question is asked (instead of barging in and blurting out a pithy religious answer) gives the Master Teacher an opportunity to overhear and answer for Himself, just as He did that day in Matthew's home.

We all must practice a spiritual conversation that has enough pauses for Jesus to interrupt. The discourse of our lives is full of unanswerable questions.

Let Jesus interrupt and show who He is, not just who you *think* He is. Our answers offer a limited view of Him. To confine the infinite in finite terms is silly. To attempt explaining omniscience with our limited breadth of understanding is equally unhelpful. God is capable of defending His position when He so chooses. He is unruffled by scrutiny and undaunted by interrogation.

Let Him be God, and you can focus on being His follower. When you are asked a tough question about the one you serve, pause, look toward the Master, and listen for His voice. God is always listening, and He will always answer a sincere questioner. You and I, as His disciples, are often questioned, and we should be prepared to offer good answers. But don't let your good answer simply placate a questioner when Christ Himself could offer the best and most satisfying answer. He will reveal Himself to those who wish to see, and He will speak to those who want to hear.

And one glimpse, one picture of Christ, is worth a thousand of our words.

> *When you are brought before synagogues, rulers and*
> *authorities, do not worry about how you will defend*
> *yourselves or what you will say, for the Holy Spirit*
> *will teach you at that time what you should say*
> *(Luke 12:11-12).*

◗ What's Percolating in Me: My Response

_____

_____

_____

_____

◗ Spill the Beans: My Prayer

_____

_____

_____

_____

◗ Thanks a Latte! My Praise

_____

_____

_____

_____

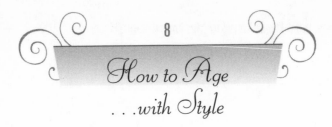

8
How to Age
. . .*with Style*

IN A *NEWSWEEK* ARTICLE, BILLY GRAHAM was quoted as saying, "All my life I've been taught how to die, but no one ever taught me how to grow old."

I, however, have had a teacher, a lifelong tutorial in how to do just that—how to grow old with style and substance. My teacher? My grandfather, Lawson Jolly Sr.

My family gathered in Clarkston, Georgia, on December 15 to lay his body to rest. He was 100 years old. Well, really, a hundred and a half. My brother David put it best when he called Papa our rock star and us his groupies.

Papa was born in 1907 and lived through World Wars I and II, the Korean Conflict, Vietnam, and our latest Middle Eastern conflicts and war. During his lifetime, 18 American presidents held office.

He seemed to grow old so slowly and negligibly that I forgot he would actually finally pass away. He just didn't seem to age. At one of our Christmas gatherings, when he was a sprightly 97, he challenged my brothers, husband, and boys to a push-up contest!

My dad presided over his funeral service. In the chill of the damp Atlanta air, I listened as my father recounted his best memories of his father.

My favorite story was one I never tire hearing. He recounted how he and Papa went on a mission trip to Korea many years ago. Because the Korean people so respect age, Papa (who was in his seventies) was selected to meet with a particularly stubborn elderly Korean gentleman whom the missionary had been trying to reach.

Papa and the missionary trekked three miles up a mountain to find the older gentleman, and after they greeted him, the aged Korean made it clear he wasn't interested.

Well, at that, Papa said; "Old man, sit down. I came all the way from America and walked three miles up this mountain just to tell you how much God loves you, and you're going to listen to me!"

The old man did just that. He sat down, listened, and received the message of Christ. Papa really was a rock star.

Someone once said, "Old age is the most unexpected of all the things that can happen to a man." Sometimes I wonder if Papa never expected to grow old and therefore never did. He lived with luster and style and loved with abandon. He was funny and a man of faith, and I will miss him terribly. A hundred years wasn't enough time to have Papa here.

If Papa could give a final word, I have a feeling it would sound a little like what Robert Frost wisely said: "In three words I can sum up everything I've learned about life. *It goes on.*"

Time moves forward even when a part of my heart is buried in Clarkston, Georgia. Life goes on, and it's up to us to march right along with it, redeeming each moment. Then maybe someday, someone will look at our lives and say, "She was my rock star, and I was her groupie."

> *And we desire that each one of you show the same*
> *diligence so as to realize the full assurance of hope*
> *until the end (Hebrews 6:11 NASB).*

❧ What's Percolating in Me: My Response

_____

_____

_____

❧ Spill the Beans: My Prayer

_____

_____

_____

❧ Thanks a Latte! My Praise

_____

_____

_____

ONE EVENING HERMAN MELVILLE, the author of *Moby Dick*, was visiting his friend and fellow novelist Nathaniel Hawthorne at his Massachusetts home. As you might imagine, the evening was filled with friendship and colorful storytelling.

Melville recounted to Hawthorne and his wife the harrowing adventures he had experienced while on a voyage in the South Seas. With exuberant gestures and lyrical tone of voice, he intricately described one particularly frightening battle between two warring island tribes. The Hawthornes were held captive by the vivid tale he wove with his words.

Several days after their evening together, the two authors met at Melville's house. At one point in their conversation, Hawthorne asked, "Could you bring out that club? I'd like to see it again."

"Club?" asked a bewildered Melville. "What club?"

"The one you were swinging about your head while you told us about the island battle."

Still confused, Melville assured his friend that he had no club.

"Of course you did," persisted Hawthorne. "I distinctly recall it. So does my wife. You brought that club back from the South Seas. It was black and carved."

The confusion finally gave way to clarity. It became obvious what had happened. Melville's storytelling had been so vivid, so compelling, and so totally enthralling that the Hawthornes really thought they had seen the club that Melville had only used words to illustrate.

Storytelling is one of the most powerful tools you and I possess. Story is a kind of incarnation, giving form to what was once invisible and lending voice to what was once inaudible. Storytelling reveals meaning without overtly defining it.

Storytelling was the method Jesus most frequently used to communicate abstract truths. He constructed concrete pictures through words and phrases. He drew out emotions and gave body to once unformed hopes with His parables. His masterful storytelling always drew a crowd and equipped His listeners with heavenly truth wrapped in earthly pictures.

Like Melville, and more importantly, like Jesus, we too are powerful in our communication when we engage in storytelling. It draws a memorable picture for our listeners that they do not soon forget. Mere words, lists, and pontifications are often lost after they are spoken. But not so with story.

I will always remember my editor's advice when I wrote my first book. She told me to show my reader what I want them to know, rather than tell them. It is so true. How often have you left a speaking event and forgotten the three points and Bible references you just heard (or even worse, you *spoke*)?

Even if we really appreciate those points and Scriptures, they are still hard to recall. But we're not likely to forget the pictures drawn in our minds by a masterful storyteller. When the story is recalled, the truth represented by that story is also recalled. As Philip Gerard said, "It's human nature to love a story and hate a lecture."

Stories often illustrate points better than simply stating the points themselves because if the story is well spoken, the point often need not be stated at all; the listeners contemplate what they've heard and figure out the point independently. The more the hearers do, the more they will get out of your story.

So my friends, show, don't just tell. Draw vivid word pictures for all to see as you communicate lasting truths. Virginia Woolf wrote, "How splendid it is to unfurl one's sail and blow straight ahead on the gust of great storytelling."

A word aptly spoken is like apples of gold
in settings of silver (Proverbs 25:11).

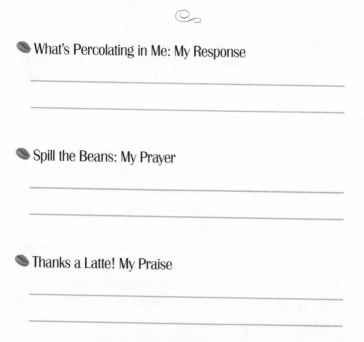

What's Percolating in Me: My Response

_____

_____

Spill the Beans: My Prayer

_____

_____

Thanks a Latte! My Praise

_____

_____

10

Every Day Is Jamaica

"If you could see just one thing for one moment, what would it be?"

I paused, pondering the radio interviewer's question.

"I'd reject the whole offer," I replied. "For me, it would be like Lay's Potato Chips…you can't eat just one."

The interviewer laughed as I continued, "I'd hesitate to choose one thing because I'd be afraid of later regretting my choice. I'd fear that a moment of sight might awaken something within me that has long been at rest under the blanket of contentment. I'd be afraid to arouse the desire to see."

The interviewer sighed and moved to the next query.

Yet days later, the question still haunted me. It nagged me and began to erode away my fortress of contentment. What made my state of mind all the worse, however, was the fact that I had just lost my cane. Actually, it had been missing for a week, and every day without it I had grown more and more frustrated. I was also in the midst of redoing my office, so all the furniture and files were in disarray. That can make even a sighted person grumpy.

Bottom line, I was tired of being blind. Sick of it. I wanted a vacation from blindness.

Just before the interview that morning, my prayer had been, "Lord, I know my healing hasn't been part of Your plan so far, but could You just give me a week? Just a week in Jamaica without blindness? Then I could come home rested and be able to be blind again for another ten years."

I guess that's why the interview question felt like the sting of a bandage being torn away too quickly. I didn't want to be able to see for a moment. *I wanted to see.*

The next day I showed up at church, my grumpy state intact. I wasn't mad at God or even carrying around a portable pity party. I was just tired, worn out.

After church, a friend introduced me to someone I had been wanting to meet. His name is Bobby Smith—a smart, funny man in his early fifties who oozes with attitude. Bobby lost his sight from a gunshot wound while on duty as a Louisiana law enforcement officer.

Bobby was only in his thirties when he became totally blind. He described his blindness like a blackness he'd never experienced before. "There's no darkness like it," he said.

He inquired of my sight loss. I told him I still had a little light perception. In other words, I could tell when it was daylight.

Bobby sighed. It was a sigh of remembrance. A sigh of pleasure. A sigh of loss.

It was also a sigh that sent Jennifer Rothschild on a little journey. In the blink of an eye, my mind raced backward along the path of discontentment I had traveled all week. And suddenly I became incredibly grateful.

I can still perceive light. I can turn my face in its direction. God has not taken that from me. I open my blinds before I go to bed at night so that the morning sun will fill my window frame and flood across my face. I feel the warmth and perceive at least something.

For now, anyway. I know that someday, as for Bobby, there may be no light at all for me. The shades of gray may all fade to black.

As I considered Bobby's experience with utter darkness, I realized I have little about which to be grumpy. It dawned on me that I've actually been in Jamaica all along. The little light I enjoy *is* my Jamaica, and I need to let that remind me of my current blessings instead of preoccupying me with my potential loss.

Gratitude for what I have, rather than grumpiness because of what I've lost, will truly give me strength for each sunrise… even if I can't see it.

In this, I felt God's touch. No one else knew my frustration. No one else knew my heartache. God did. God knew that only a blind man could help me see God's light. So, my friend, what is your Jamaica? Thank God for it. Open the eyes of your heart and let the light of gratitude brighten your dark places.

I am the light of the world. Whoever follows me
will never walk in darkness, but will have the
light of life (John 8:12).

What's Percolating in Me: My Response

_____

_____

_____

_____

Spill the Beans: My Prayer

_____

_____

_____

_____

Thanks a Latte! My Praise

_____

_____

_____

_____

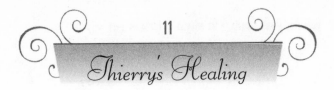

11
Thierry's Healing

THERE WAS ONCE A VERY SPECIAL EASTER SUNDAY, and I wanted to spend it in Tallahassee, Florida, worshipping with my friend Thierry. You see, Thierry, Diane, and their children are friends from our former church. I met Thierry when he was a new believer. From that day to this, he has always had such zeal and enthusiasm for the Lord—he has always lifted my spirit and made me laugh.

In late 1999, however, Thierry was diagnosed with a stage 4 glioblastoma—a brain tumor—and the prognosis was not good. In fact, one doctor informed him that only 2 out of every 100 people with this condition survive.

Words could not express our shock and sadness. For Thierry, the year of his diagnosis was filled with prayer, medical treatment, diet, and surgery. And for those of us who loved him, it was a year spent on our knees. The months passed with difficulty and took us through Christmas and into the year 2000. As Easter approached that year, I anticipated the results of Thierry's most recent MRI.

The news came late on a Monday night: "No tumor detected."

That Easter Sunday, the pastor might just as well have stepped aside when Thierry stood to testify to resurrection power. That day no one would praise more loudly than he, no one would celebrate more deeply, and no one would bow with more humility.

It occurs to me that when our world is as dark as the inside of a tomb, God has a way of rolling away the stone, flooding our lives with the light of hope. All along, Thierry's world was bright, knowing that his healing would come either on this side or on the other.

And isn't that the assurance of Easter? Death has no sting.

This Sunday, you and I should celebrate as deeply and praise as loudly because we are not unlike Thierry. Don't ever forget that your very life was snatched from certain death and brought into peace and wholeness because of Resurrection Sunday.

> *I will sing of the LORD's great love forever;*
> *with my mouth I will make*
> *your faithfulness known (Psalm 89:1).*

What's Percolating in Me: My Response

Spill the Beans: My Prayer

Thanks a Latte! My Praise

12

Thy Word Have I Hid in My Purse

I WAS GIVEN A HIGHLY VALUABLE, life changing, totally unexpected gift at a conference in Montgomery, Alabama. After finishing my first message of the weekend, a lovely woman named Carol introduced herself to me. After our introductions, she grasped my hand and placed within it a small piece of equipment wrapped with dangling ear phones.

Before I could even ask, Carol began to explain. She told me that she, like me, lost most of her vision as a teenage girl. She quickly skipped through her inspiring story and then instructed me to place the earphones in my ears. As I did, she then reviewed the keypad on the face of the tiny unit, and told me to push one of the buttons. I followed her instruction and then, as I began to listen, I promptly forgot that I was standing with a new friend named Carol in an auditorium. I had no idea I was in Alabama, and if you had asked me at that very moment to introduce myself, I might very well have forgotten my own name.

Why? Because I was transported to a place of pure pleasure. I was enraptured by a voice belonging to someone named "Precise Pete," and what I was listening to awakened a tender impulse and a cherished desire within me.

Pete read from the book of John in a digital voice, but to me, it was music. It was the lyric of my life and the melody of my heart, and it was small enough to hold in my hand…which naturally would make it easier to hide in my heart.

The little device was called the Bible Courier. It was the size of a deck of cards, and it contained the whole Bible. I took out the earphones, exclaiming how wonderful and handy the Courier was, and reluctantly handed it back to Carol.

"No," she protested, "it's for you! God led me to give it to you. It's a gift."

I tried to refuse—even though I wanted that little Bible with all my heart. "You can't give me this," I said. "You need it! I'll buy my own when I get home." I tried to convince her, but to no avail. I knew I was contending with a determined blind woman, and since I am one too, I gratefully accepted her generosity.

By the second leg of my flight home, I had listened to several books of the Old Testament, totally ignored my traveling companion, and mastered the new little Bible that was small enough to hide in my purse.

I wish I could put into words how much I love this new digital Bible. I wish I could explain how grateful I am to God and Carol for opening up my world with His Word.

The Courier gave my thoughts wings and a reason to fly.

You see, I am grateful I can listen to the Word on my computer, but it's way too heavy to travel with. I love having the Bible on CD and cassette, but those formats are much harder to navigate. It's almost impossible to find specific verses.

This format, though, gives me instant access and easy

navigation, and it eliminates any excuse I could have ever had for neglecting the Word.

But I have never wanted to neglect the Word anyway. I have loved it since I was a child. And now I listen to it all the time. I sit in church with the earphones in my ear and the Courier in my purse. I wash dishes while listening to Hosea with the Courier clipped to my pocket. I fold laundry, walk the treadmill, and fall asleep listening to the Word. Precise Pete and I have become fast friends. How could I ever ask for more?

John Adams once told his son, John Quincy, that he would never be alone with a "poet in his pocket." Well, I say I will never be alone with the Word in my purse, or better yet, in my heart. It has quenched a thirst deep within my spirit that I never realized was so intense.

To my sighted friends I say, please don't take for granted the opportunity you have to open your Bible most anytime, most anywhere, and read to your heart's content. Don't willingly allow yourself to be in the dark regardless of how well your eyes may see. You need the light of God's Word as desperately as I do. Carry it with you. Hide it in your purse. Tuck it away in your heart. It will give your thoughts wings and a reason to fly.*

The entrance of His Word really does bring light.

> *The entrance of Your words gives light;*
> *It gives understanding to the simple*
> *(Psalm 119:130 NKJV).*

---

* My deepest thanks go to Carol, my sister in Christ, and the wonderful folks at Lutheran Braille Evangelism Association, who produce and make available the Bible Courier.

14

A Little Note
on Sovereignty

IN MY *WALKING BY FAITH* BIBLE STUDY, I make this statement: "God is in control of Satan and his actions; Satan can never act outside the limits God sets."

A woman wrote me asking me to clarify that statement. Apparently a member of her study group had a huge struggle with the first clause of the sentence: "God is in control of Satan and his actions." The phrase made her feel uneasy because it suggested to her that Satan was God's puppet, and it put bad things in God's hands and His control instead of Satan's.

Looking back, I wish I had phrased that statement a little differently. Maybe something like this: "God is sovereign over Satan and his actions."

To be sovereign means God has ultimate power and authority over everything and everyone. That is certainly true. Yet His authority often expresses itself in a willingness to allow that which His power could prevent, such as suffering and evil.

Satan is not God's puppet, acting at His bidding. He is no more God's puppet than we are. In God's sovereignty and benevolence, He allowed free will to exist. The existence of free will permits choice, and choice ushers in the possibility for sin and evil. In God's sovereignty, He allows evil, but He also sets the boundaries for evil.

When I say "God is in control of Satan and his actions," I'm saying that God has ultimate authority over everything that happens in your life. And that's not the same as saying He controls each action of Satan's—or yours or mine, for that matter.

The most clear and obvious example of God's sovereignty over Satan is in the first chapter of Job. There Satan came to God requesting permission to afflict the patriarch. The fact is, even though Satan is consumed by hatred and completely motivated by evil, he cannot touch us without God's permission.

When you read through the entire book of Job, you find at the end that God was working all the while in His servant's life (see Job 42:5-6). You see that just as Joseph's brothers meant their actions for evil but God used them for good, Satan ultimately does the work of God.

So for me, I choose to accept God's authority, depend on His power, and trust His benevolence and sovereignty.

It isn't always easy, but it's always right.

> *Oh, the depth of the riches of the wisdom and*
> *knowledge of God!*
> *How unsearchable his judgments,*
> *and his paths beyond tracing out!*
> *"Who has known the mind of the Lord?*
> *Or who has been his counselor?"*
> *"Who has ever given to God,*
> *that God should repay him?"*

For from him and through him and to him
are all things.
To him be the glory forever! Amen
(Romans 11:33-36).

❧

🫘 What's Percolating in Me: My Response

_____

_____

_____

🫘 Spill the Beans: My Prayer

_____

_____

_____

🫘 Thanks a Latte! My Praise

_____

_____

_____

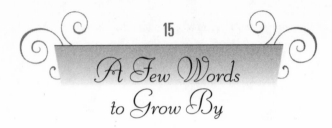

15

A Few Words
to Grow By

MY FRIEND JONI ASKED ME TO contribute to a special book she was compiling for her daughter Hannah's thirteenth birthday. As a mother of sons, it was fun for me to offer her a few words to grow by.

And it got me thinking.

During this spring season, when my mailbox is full of graduation announcements and wedding invitations, these words may apply to a number of young women. So what I offered to Hannah, I offer to you too.

When you realize how powerful emotions can be...

Remember always to elevate your faith above your feelings. Why? Because that which you elevate highly will govern you. Feelings change, but the precepts of faith are unchanging. Feelings change, but truth changes you. Always allow yourself to be governed by that which is eternal rather than that which is so temporary.

For we walk by faith, not by sight
(2 Corinthians 5:7).

When you come to a sudden bump in the road...

Never allow your life circumstances to *define* you. Instead, let them *refine* you. Hard things are like heavenly sandpaper on your life. God uses them to shape and mold you into a work of art. When you feel the pressure of trials, remember that God won't allow them to crush you; He intends for them to make you beautiful.

> We are afflicted in every way, but not crushed;
> perplexed, but not despairing; persecuted,
> but not forsaken; struck down, but not destroyed;
> always carrying about in the body the dying
> of Jesus, that the life of Jesus also may
> be manifested in our body
> (2 Corinthians 4:8-9 NASB).

When you feel afraid...

Always exercise courage even when you don't feel confident. Courage is a choice; confidence is a feeling. Remember that courage and confidence are not the same thing. Be brave, my sweet Hannah, for bravery broadens you. Fear limits you.

Ask God to help you overcome earthly fear by developing reverence for Him. The only fear that brings you wisdom is the fear of God. Fear Him, reverence Him, and nothing else will shake you.

For God has not given us a spirit of timidity,
but of power and love and discipline
(2 Timothy 1:7 NASB).

When you don't like what you see in the mirror...

Look into the mirror of God's Word. When you do, you will see how incredibly beautiful and valuable you are. Merely glance into the bathroom mirror, but gaze into the mirror of God's Word. It will always show you the truth because it is the truth. Trust God's opinion of you more than you trust others' opinions—or even your own opinion of yourself.

Only the Word of God is eternal and worthy of your gaze. To look into the mirror of God's Word is to see the face of God, and in doing so, you are better equipped to see who you really are.

And Hannah, you are beautiful and dearly loved.

My friends, plant these words deep in the heart of a young woman that you love, and may they be words that grow into sturdy and steadfast character.

Then the King will desire your beauty.
Because He is your Lord, bow down to Him
(Psalm 45:11 NASB).

What's Percolating in Me: My Response

_____

_____

_____

_____

Spill the Beans: My Prayer

_____

_____

_____

_____

Thanks a Latte! My Praise

_____

_____

_____

_____

16

Sing to the Orchestra

I JUST LOVE IT WHEN the choir and orchestra put on a grand concert at our home church. What a fabulous evening. I remember a particularly special night featuring gospel quartets singing about their first day in heaven and contemporary soloists singing "I Can Only Imagine."

The whole night made me want to turn in my seat so I was facing east because I just knew that Jesus Himself was going to split the sky that very night and rapture us into His presence.

The highlight of the evening for me, however, had to be when the choir sang to the orchestra. At one point in the concert, our worship pastor, Dr. Joe Crider, turned to the congregation and began to tell of how faithful our talented church orchestra had been for more than 20 years. He spoke of how they consistently and skillfully rehearse every week and never fail to move us to heights of worship each Sunday morning.

His voice began to break as he concluded. "So tonight, we as the congregation and choir, and I as your grateful leader, want you to lay down your instruments and just listen as we attempt to say thank you."

The piano played softly as a soloist came on stage. A beautiful tenor voice began to sweetly sing "Thank You" by Ray Boltz. The beautiful lyrics thank others for giving to the Lord.

I could hear sniffles from the orchestra pit, and I'm sure that eyes in the congregation were moist as well. What a beautiful surprise for those dedicated musicians to receive, and what an appropriate honor.

It got me to thinking. What about the orchestra in my life and ministry? Maybe they could use a song or two of thanks.

We all have our orchestras, don't we? They are frequently unseen, unheralded people who contribute so much to our success and joy but just seem to fade into the background most of the time. I'm thinking of those who quietly support, consistently follow, and humbly serve so that the music of our lives and ministry might be beautiful.

I think of Kathryn McCall, my wonderful assistant. She left a lucrative job in the banking industry to join God in ministry wherever He led. Boy, am I grateful He led her to me! She works tirelessly, cheerfully, and skillfully. I depend on her so and wouldn't be able to do many of the things God calls me to do without her. And besides all that, she's loads of fun!

Another member of the orchestra is Karen True, my writing and research assistant. Abounding in talent as she does, she also serves as my newsletter designer, website design consultant, wardrobe consultant, interior decorator, computer coach, and best girlfriend. So much of what I do is possible because of her faithful commitment to God and me.

Of course, the real wind beneath my "sings" is my very own Dr. Phil—my awesome husband. WomensMinistry.NET, Java with Jennifer, and Fresh Grounded Faith Conferences wouldn't even exist if not for his insight, drive, and commitment. He has steadied and challenged me through the years of our growing ministry and been the single catalyst for expanding our vision.

There are others, like Billie, Robyne, and Alisa who add so much. And things would really be out of tune without our gifted son Clayton. He is our webmaster, and he manfully handles all things that require geek intervention. Without him, we wouldn't function on the Web or in our office nearly as well.

So this has now served as one verse of the song I sing to my orchestra. Thank you for being willing to give to the Lord. I may be on stage, but you are part of the unseen foundation upon which I stand.

So my friend, tune up and tune in. Do you need to sing to an orchestra today?

> *I commend to you our sister Phoebe, a servant of the church in Cenchrea. I ask you to receive her in the Lord in a way worthy of the saints and to give her any help she may need from you, for she has been a great help to many people, including me. Greet Priscilla and Aquila, my fellow workers in Christ Jesus. They risked their lives for me. Not only I but all the churches of the Gentiles are grateful to them…*
>
> *Greet Mary, who worked very hard for you…*
>
> *Greet Tryphena and Tryphosa, those women who work hard in the Lord. Greet my dear friend Persis, another woman who has worked very hard in the Lord (Romans 16:1-3,6,12).*

What's Percolating in Me: My Response

_____

_____

_____

_____

Spill the Beans: My Prayer

_____

_____

_____

_____

Thanks a Latte! My Praise

_____

_____

_____

_____

17

Stolen Time

I JUST RETURNED HOME from a three-day ministry trip, where the strangest thing occurred. Time was stolen from me, but I ended up getting it back. Here's what happened…

Sunday morning I went through my usual routine of getting dressed, methodically placing everything I have with me in the exact same locations regardless of what hotel I may be staying in. For example, I always place my jewelry in the nightstand drawer and my cosmetics against the right wall of the bathroom vanity. It's just one of the things I do to make sightless travel a little less stressful.

But in my haste on Sunday morning, I laid my talking watch on the bathroom counter next to my makeup. I actually hesitated as I did so (you know the feeling…*I may regret this*) but reassured myself that I'd make a mental note to get it later, and scurried out the door. (Beware of those little mental notes!)

Later, after four meetings and one worship service, I dragged myself back into the hotel room, got ready for bed, and reached for my watch.

And it wasn't there.

I felt all around the counter because housekeeping had tidied up and perhaps moved the watch. But I couldn't lay my hand on it. I retraced my steps and again checked all around the counter, on the floor, and even in my makeup bag. No watch.

At this point I enlisted the private detective services of my husband. Phil searched like a bloodhound—under beds, in drawers, atop furniture. He emptied my purse, unzipped and searched all our bags, and then announced, "It's gone."

I was *so* upset. Had someone actually stolen my watch, or was I merely losing my mind? Neither option appealed to me as I despondently crawled into bed.

You see, this really wasn't about missing jewelry. In my blindness, a talking watch is one of the stars by which I navigate. My watch represents more than the time of day. It has a lot to do with my sense of independence and autonomy. That's what had been stolen, and that's why I was upset.

Before my talking watch days, I hated always asking everyone else, "What time is it?" or "How much longer until we leave?" I loved the freedom of pressing a button and having a distinguished male voice in a contrived British accent announce the time to me. And now, during this busy ministry event, I would have no idea what time it was. My missing watch sent me rapidly from the liberty of independence to the confines of dependence.

I tossed and turned all night, awoke the next morning, and asked my husband, "What time is it?" about 87 times while I got dressed.

At the end of the day, I pulled my final pantsuit from my suitcase to wear the following morning. As I unfurled the pants, something came loose and fell to the floor. I reached down, grabbed it, and squealed, "My watch!"

There was no mental note in my memory bank that read, "You placed your watch within the intricate folds of your taupe suit." No, I racked my brain and still came up with no explanation. (I know very well where I had left it.) Perhaps it had been temporarily borrowed by someone who felt guilty and later put it back in my room—or perhaps I really am losing my mind!

But whatever the case, I'm so very thankful it's back because with its return came my sense of independence.

That's a story about a possibly stolen and thankfully restored watch. An open and shut case, you might say. But it isn't quite so simple when the stolen item isn't a watch, but *time itself.*

When we misplace time in our own lives, we lose considerably more than just minutes and hours. We lose a little freedom. When we are careless with our schedules, allow ourselves to become over-committed, or neglect priorities, we lose some of our freedom to say yes to God and sit at His feet.

Don't let time be stolen from you, and for heaven's sake, don't misplace it because you're too hurried or neglectful. You may lose more than just the moments. You might also lose some priceless opportunities.

Therefore be careful how you walk, not as unwise
men but as wise, making the most of your time,
because the days are evil. So then do not be foolish,
but understand what the will of the Lord is
(Ephesians 5:15–17 NASB).

What's Percolating in Me: My Response

_____

_____

_____

_____

Spill the Beans: My Prayer

_____

_____

_____

_____

Thanks a Latte! My Praise

_____

_____

_____

_____

18

Strolling with My Hero

IT WAS A SPECIAL DREAM-COME-TRUE when I had the privilege of appearing on a TV show with my hero, Joni Eareckson Tada.

She made her way into my heart when I was a teenage girl. In fact, the summer before I lost my sight, her book, *Joni,* was the last book I read with my own eyes. Only God could have known how each word she wrote would shine as a guiding light of hope, warming and inspiring me to face my coming darkness. Over the years, I have heard her on radio and TV, listened to all her books, and admired her from afar.

It's no surprise then, that I arrived at the studio dizzy with excitement. I was going to be with Joni and talk to her! When we were finally in the green room before the show, I made my way over to her, introduced myself, and told her I was a shameless fan and that I was honored to meet her.

She laughed, telling me she'd read my first book and had my CDs.

In those priceless moments before the show, we chatted and laughed, and I found her every bit as enchanting and wise as I had imagined her to be.

Afterward, Joni suggested that all of the guests go out and

pray with those in the studio audience who had lingered after the show. "Grab my chair, Jennifer," she said. "Let's go!"

And don't you know I did just as she instructed. I held on as she rolled toward the audience, and I kept saying to myself, *Jennifer is walking with Joni, Joni is with Jennifer.* Next to her, I was beside myself! Just as she had spiritually guided me for years, she was now guiding me physically. Cool.

We arrived in the circle of audience members, and her assistant held a microphone in front of her. "Rather than praying," she said, "let's all sing 'Amazing Grace' together."

She led the first verse as we all sang along, reverence and gratitude settling over our harmony. Then she paused before she led the second verse and said, "I want Jennifer to sing the 'Through many dangers, toils, and snares' verse as we hum quietly."

Her assistant handed me the mike and I began to sing. But here's the deal...I was panicking inside because I wasn't sure I knew the words! I thought to myself, *Oh, why couldn't she have chosen the 'ten thousand years' verse?* I have trouble remembering my children's names most days, much less the lyrics to a little-known verse of "Amazing Grace."

But Joni, my hero, had asked me to sing, and sing I did.

Thankfully, each word came to mind as I prayerfully sang. And then it hit me. As I stood next to my hero singing about God's grace, I had instinctively raised my hand in praise. But I was one of the only guests on the show who *could* lift my hand to God. You see, Joni is a quadriplegic, so she can't lift her hand in praise. Two of the incredible guests on the show that day, Nick and Tony, didn't have arms and hands to lift to God, as they had been born without limbs.

And in that moment, I was overwhelmed with the reality of what I have rather than what I've lost. Even in her stillness next to me, Joni showed me the privilege I possess in the ability to raise my hand to heaven and kneel in gratitude before God.

Perhaps you should do the same today. Lift your hands to heaven and thank God for what He has given you...for what you have. Bow before Him and thank Him even for what you have lost.

Thank you, Lord, and thank you, Joni.

You have given me the heritage of those who fear
your name (Psalm 61:5).

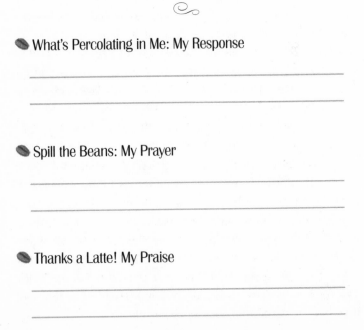

What's Percolating in Me: My Response

_____

_____

Spill the Beans: My Prayer

_____

_____

Thanks a Latte! My Praise

_____

_____

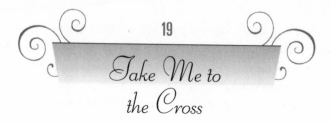

19

Take Me to the Cross

I SETTLED INTO MY DESK CHAIR to listen to the day's e-mails, and the first one I opened was from a young man named Greg. He and I were introduced several years earlier when he first wrote me with the sad news, "I have cancer and I have faith, and I don't know how to have both."

After a few months of corresponding, his cancer was in remission, and our e-mails grew fewer and fewer.

That particular summer day though, the first line of his e-mail read, "The cancer's back, and I'm afraid."

I was so sad for Greg. My first response was, "O God, why?" I went to the next e-mail. It was from a woman who had been at one of my conferences a few weeks earlier. At the conference, she was pregnant. She wrote to tell me her baby had been born—stillborn—and she was devastated. So was I.

My tears began to fall. "God, why?"

I left my computer and went to my piano with more questions than answers and a heart heavy with compassion and helplessness. As I began to play, wondering why God allows these things, I glanced heavenward and asked, "Why cancer? Why stillborn babies? Why blindness? It seems so unfair."

Suddenly the shadow of the cross fell on my questions. As I saw that place of ultimate unfairness through my tears, my question was no longer, "Why suffering?" but rather, "Why grace? Why peace? Why love?"

When I am tempted to ask why, as if the existence of pain is an unfairness in this life, I need only to look to the cross, where true unfairness and the ultimate unanswered question remains. Why does God grant us grace, forgiveness, peace, love? It's not fair that we should receive such benevolence from Him.

As a result of my contemplation, I wrote these lyrics to remind me to embrace the mystery of faith rather than allow unanswered questions to keep me from intimacy with God—to help me embrace what I can't understand, and in doing so, encounter Him.

That's what I want for Greg in his renewed struggle with cancer, for the precious woman who lost her baby, and for you too, whatever your hurts and unanswered questions might be today.

TAKE ME TO THE CROSS

He said the cancer's back and he's afraid
He wonders why
So do I.
Now his greatest battle is against his fear
It's so unclear
He wonders why.
The God who heals
Won't reveal Himself
In ways we understand.
She said her baby never had a chance to breathe
So she grieves

So do I.
She struggles with the bitterness and loss
While she looks to the cross
And she cries.
In the mystery we trust, we adjust, and
wonder why.
Oh, take me to the cross where You cried
my tears
Hide me in Your tomb, crucify my fears.
I'll praise You with my pain though the
mystery remains
You are a God who cries, You are a Savior
who died
And I can trust You with why.
So I travel down this bumpy road called faith
And with blind eyes,
I still try
To embrace all that I can't understand
Like Your kind plan, Your merciful plan.
I'm not angered, I am anchored. Yet I feel
weightless, I am hateless.
Since You took me to the cross
And cried each of my tears.
Hid me in Your tomb, crucified my fears.
I praise You with my pain though the
mystery remains
You are a God who cries, You are a Savior
who died
And I will trust You with why.
I'll ask You why, why, this grace?
Why this peace?

Why, why, this love?
I praise You with my pain though the
    mystery remains
You are a God who cries, You are a Savior
    who died
And I can trust You with why.

⌒

We have depended on God's grace, not on our own
human wisdom (2 Corinthians 1:12 NLT).

⌒

🫘 What's Percolating in Me: My Response

_____

_____

🫘 Spill the Beans: My Prayer

_____

_____

🫘 Thanks a Latte! My Praise

_____

_____

20

Tell Me Why

I LISTENED AS DEBBIE RECOUNTED a story of a recent family vacation.

She, her husband, and their two sons had been on a summer Colorado adventure. She laughed as she told about their growing disenchantment with fast food during the trip. You know what it's like when traveling…the taco establishment just doesn't ring your bell after several subsequent visits. The golden arches lose their glimmer, and the king of burgers has to step down from the throne.

Hungry for a good, well balanced, healthy meal, Debbie's family sought out a local diner that advertised home-cooked meals. The fragrance of pot roast and potatoes, freshly brewed coffee, and warm apple crisp was inviting to the weary travelers. They ordered their heart's desire when the waitress arrived. But when she returned with their meals, they were astounded by the portions. They were *huge*. At first glance, it looked as though there was enough food on just one of the plates to feed the entire family.

Mom and Dad ate about half of their dinners and then, miserably, pushed their plates away. Their youngest son, a strapping teenager, was able to put away slightly more than his parents, but eventually he too surrendered, pushing aside his plate.

The oldest son, Dustin, however, was just getting warmed up. He had easily finished his own dinner, and was looking longingly at the lovely leftovers on his family's plates.

Dustin is a precious young man with Down syndrome, and he loves to eat. Debbie knew that this setting was not the place to prohibit Dustin from engaging in one of his favorite pastimes, so when he asked for his brother's leftovers, Mom consented.

After Dustin had polished off both his and his brother's dinner, the waitress arrived and asked, "May I take your plate?"

Dustin simply shook his head. He wasn't finished. He then proceeded to finish up his dad's lukewarm leftovers. The waitress returned once again. "May I take your plate?"

"No," Dustin said.

He then directed his fork and his intentions toward his mother's plate and began to eat. The waitress returned one last time and flatly inquired "May I take your plate now?"

Irritated but reconciled to his fate, Dustin finally agreed. No sooner had the waitress gathered the empty plates and turned to leave for the kitchen did Dustin announce to his family, "That waitress needs to get her own food."

I laughed at Debbie's sweet story. But later I thought about some of the parenting implications of the incident. As moms and dads, we try to set good examples for our children, modeling good and godly behavior for those who observe our lives—just as Debbie and her family had modeled proper restaurant behavior for Dustin. But often simply modeling isn't enough; sometimes we need to explain why we do the things we do.

Obviously, Dustin, with his special needs, didn't understand why the waitress wanted his leftovers. He only knew that was customary behavior for a waitress in a restaurant.

In the same way, our children may not really understand why we do the things we do as believers. Why do we pray before meals? Why do we forgive when someone else was clearly in the wrong? Why do we continue to view issues as black-and-white when our culture sees only gray? Why do we never stop hoping and trusting regardless of the circumstances? Why?

Setting a good example and trying to model godly behavior is one thing. But for lasting impact, we must also make clear the godly basis for our behavior.

In Deuteronomy 6, Moses urges the dads and moms about to enter the promised land to do more than hang a cross-stitched copy of the Ten Commandments on their dining room walls.

> "You shall love the LORD your God with all your heart and with all your soul and with all your might. These words, which I am commanding you today, shall be on your heart. You shall teach them diligently to your sons and shall talk of them when you sit in your house and when you walk by the way and when you lie down and when you rise up" (vv. 5-7 NASB).

In other words, don't just model a godly lifestyle—talk about it. Explain it. Hash it out. Make it a daily topic of conversation. Make it interesting and engaging. Moses was saying, "It's fine if these things are on your heart. That's good. But you need to take the next step and teach while you are modeling."

Though a godly life speaks volumes to those who observe,

your example is not the same as an explanation. So be ready, my friend, to give an answer for the hope that is in you.

Preach the Word; be prepared in season and out of season; correct, rebuke and encourage—with great patience and careful instruction (2 Timothy 4:2-3).

What's Percolating in Me: My Response

_____

_____

_____

Spill the Beans: My Prayer

_____

_____

_____

Thanks a Latte! My Praise

_____

_____

_____

21

In the Midst of Mystery

A STILLBORN BABY, a fatal car wreck, a freak accident...these are all mysteries that cause us anguish and raise questions in our hearts. A wayward child, a terminal disease, a terrorist attack...isn't an all-powerful God supposed to show His power by intervening in such baffling, tragic circumstances?

When a human mystery like the Bermuda Triangle or the disappearance of Amelia Earhart remains unsolved, we are intrigued, but when a divine mystery takes center stage in our lives, we can easily fall into despair.

Why? Because mysteries leave us with questions, not answers.

Unanswered questions are the unwelcome companions to human suffering. Rarely does an answer emerge from suffering. The more questions we ask, the more we seem to have.

Why won't God heal when He could? Why do the innocent suffer? How can God really be good if He allows such evil?

When an infinite God allows unanswered questions, we as finite humans tend to attribute His silence to one of several things—either He doesn't know, He doesn't care, or He really can't do anything about it.

When God engages in mystery with us, we will sometimes

create a myth to explain His "disappointing behavior" and to help us understand. We conjure up such myths because our human logic and feelings don't measure up. In so doing, however, we set up a deceitful standard. And when God doesn't meet that standard, when He doesn't clear the arbitrary height at which we've set our bar, we assume He has failed or abandoned us.

Our myths might sound like this: "If I just have enough faith, God will heal me. After all, don't I deserve His blessing? If God is powerful enough to deliver me, then He should."

The prophet Habakkuk must have struggled with (what I am calling) the failure of God. The man had questions—deep, earnest, searching questions—about suffering and justice and evil in the world. But though he sought answers from the right source, God Himself, the answers didn't turn out the way he had probably imagined.

> How long, O LORD, will I call for help, and You
> will not hear? I cry out to You, "Violence!" yet You
> do not save.

> Why do You make me see iniquity, and cause me
> to look on wickedness? Yes, destruction and vio-
> lence are before me; strife exists and contention
> arises (Habakkuk 1:2-3 NASB).

Habakkuk's three-chapter dialogue with heaven doesn't end with the neat, tidy answers the man of God had been hoping for. Instead, it ends with praise.

The prophet had been hoping that coming to God would answer all the mysteries that had been distressing him, but God left him with mysteries that were even deeper still.

Even so, he'd had an encounter with the greatness and wisdom of the living God, and that had brought him to his knees. And when he was on his knees, his world began to make sense.

The prophet's satisfaction was not in the answers he received to his questions, but rather in the *encounter with the God he had questioned*. The same is true for us. Our satisfaction and peace won't be found in having all our questions answered to our satisfaction, but rather in the encounter we have with God because of the questions. The encounter provides meaning in the mystery.

I'll be honest: I usually have more questions than answers. Yet I have peace. I live with that which I cannot understand. I daily embrace the mystery of my blindness, and in this mystery I find meaning because I find God there. As with Habakkuk, the satisfaction I experience is not in the answers I receive, but rather in spending time with my God the midst of the mystery.

Oh, my friend, I long for you to have a real, life-transforming encounter with God. May we all recognize that the "failure" we may have once assigned to God is really a failure of the myths we have unwittingly embraced. Only when we reject the myths and embrace the mystery do we begin to experience the intimacy waiting for us.

Answers never satisfy; only intimacy with God does. If you are in the midst of a painful mystery, stop seeking answers and seek God instead.

He is waiting to satisfy you with Himself.

> *Though the fig tree should not blossom,*
> *nor fruit be on the vines,*
> *the produce of the olive fail*

and the fields yield no food,
the flock be cut off from the fold
and there be no herd in the stalls,
yet I will rejoice in the LORD;
I will take joy in the God of my salvation.
GOD, the Lord, is my strength;
he makes my feet like the deer's;
he makes me tread on my high places
(Habakkuk 3:17-19 ESV).

● What's Percolating in Me: My Response

_____

_____

● Spill the Beans: My Prayer

_____

_____

● Thanks a Latte! My Praise

_____

_____

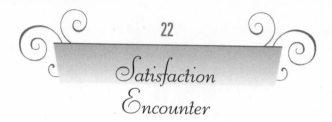

22

Satisfaction Encounter

IN THE LAST CHAPTER, I wrote about the prophet Habakkuk and how his questions finally melted into praise.

I'm reminded of another encounter with the prophet that began years ago when I was attempting to write my first book proposal and really needed help.

After working up my courage, I picked up the phone and called Karen True to see if she might have any interest in assisting me. There was a problem, though. I really didn't know Karen very well, and she didn't know me. We went to the same church, so I hoped she might recognize me.

Praying she wouldn't think I was crazy, I dialed Karen's number. Stumbling and stammering, I told her about the book proposal and how God had led me to call her. She was gracious, and our conversation ended with an agreement to meet.

Well, that began a wonderful relationship. We've researched, laughed, eaten dark chocolate, cried, traveled, and worshipped together. What began as a working relationship became a precious friendship.

A few years ago, as we began working on the *Fingerprints of God* Bible study, I began to notice some little changes in my extraordinarily sharp friend. She seemed tired most of the time—and uncharacteristically forgetful. Concerned about the changes, she visited the doctor. The tests and visits to specialists lasted all summer. When it was all said and done, we learned that Karen had cancer.

By this time, it was early fall, and the manuscript for our Bible study was due within a month. We had forged through writer's block, grappled with how to make big concepts small, and at times, felt like spectators as we watched God work through our feeble thoughts and pens.

But at that point I felt only a sinking feeling that seemed to pull every platitude I could have offered right out of my vocabulary. My heart was broken for my friend. I knew from the nature of the cancer that the prognosis was good, but I also knew that my dear friend would have a long and hard road ahead of her.

The questions and concerns began to surface in my mind. *Why Karen? Why now? We're almost done writing the Bible study. How will I finish it without her? Lord, she is my eyes on this project. We're partners; she's my friend.*

Answers from heaven? I didn't hear any at that time. What I remember looking back now was only stress, uncertainty…and determined faith.

Finally the surgery day arrived. I met Karen and her family at the hospital very early on a September morning, and we gathered around her bed for prayer.

She maintained her usual peacefulness, and I tried hard to hide my discomfort. Worry, questions, stress, and an inability to escape the general unfairness of it all weighed heavy on me. I was unsatisfied. Of course, my overachieving friend Karen does all things well and she came through the surgery and radiation great.

One year later, her cancer was completely gone, and she was soon back to her old self. Not long after that she taught an inspiring Bible class on—who else?—the prophet Habakkuk, and I was privileged to attend.

Karen offered her unique take on the prophet's struggle with the unfairness of life. She taught of Habakkuk's questioning of God. As I listened to her, I felt like the prophet that she described. As I noted earlier, the prophet's book opens with a series of questions and complaints: *How long, Lord? Why, Lord?* That was the song I had also been singing. *Why cancer? Why Karen? Why at that point in her life?*

When it came to Karen's cancer, I sought satisfaction for my questions, yet I have had few answers. But as we said a few pages back, Habakkuk's book ends with praise and confirmation. And I want the book of my life to end the very same way.

Don't ever let your questions keep you from His presence. Instead, as you ask and seek, may your searching lead you to an unforgettable encounter with your loving, sovereign God.

Oh my friend, don't despise those yet-unanswered questions in your life. They may prove to be stepping-stones toward a deepening relationship with your God—the almighty, eternal Redeemer who loves you—that goes far, far beyond any specific information you desire.

Ultimately, the needs of our soul and spirit go beyond the needs of our body and mind. When we rest in Him—His strength, His sovereignty, His infinite wisdom—we find rest that goes well beyond mere answered questions.

LORD, I have heard the report about You and I fear.
O LORD, revive Your work in the midst of the years,
In the midst of the years make it known;
In wrath remember mercy.

God comes from Teman,
And the Holy One from Mount Paran. Selah.
His splendor covers the heavens,
And the earth is full of His praise.
His radiance is like the sunlight;
He has rays flashing from His hand,
And there is the hiding of His power.
…His ways are everlasting
(Habakkuk 3:2-4,6 NASB).

☕ What's Percolating in Me: My Response

_____

_____

_____

_____

☕ Spill the Beans: My Prayer

_____

_____

_____

_____

☕ Thanks a Latte! My Praise

_____

_____

_____

_____

23

The Formula

IT'S A QUESTION I'VE BEEN ASKED many times, by strangers in interviews and by friends in casual conversation. It's also a question I've been asking of myself rather often these days.

It's a question about balance. Yes, the dreaded B-word. And it usually goes something like this: "How do you find balance as a woman in ministry?" The answer is far less simple.

I've been pondering, praying, and listening to the wisdom of mentors to try to come up with an easy answer. You know, a formula. Perhaps I could discover the perfect ratio of yes and no responses to opportunities outside the home. Or maybe the quantum balance question is answered by multiplying the ages of your children to how many hours of sleep you require divided by your ideal body weight.

The answer in my case is 1.32.

Meaning...what? I should dedicate 1 hour and 32 minutes each day to (what?). Or I should eliminate 1 hour and 32 minutes of (what?) out of my schedule.

See what I mean? I've woefully decided that there is no formula. A seasoned communicator recently told me that she simply listens to God—He tells her how often, when, and where to speak, and what and when to write.

I'm such a radical type A that I really need a little more

structure from the Lord. Something I can measure my schedule and motives against. You know, a goal. I'm convinced that if I aim at nothing, I will succeed all too well at hitting exactly that. And so my pursuit brought me through the pages of Scripture and landed me at—would you believe it?—a formula.

Or is it a goal?

Whatever it is, it's found in Micah 6:8. God says (in so many words), "Here's a way to live. It's good. It's healthy. It makes sense, and it's what I want for you." He even broke it up into three parts! So for all of us type A's who don't function well in the abstract, God made it perfectly concrete.

> He has shown you, O man, what is good;
> And what does the LORD require of you
> But to do justly,
> To love mercy,
> And to walk humbly with your God?
> (Micah 6:8 NKJV).

To be balanced, we need to *do justly*.

That means we implement fairness and rightness toward our family and ourselves as we fill in our empty calendar slots. Doing justly, we can say no sometimes in order to be fair to ourselves, our family, and our God. But notice the *do* in "do justly." Rather than pulling back and shrinking away from all demands, we utilize our limited time and resources in the most equitable way possible.

To be balanced, we must also *love mercy*.

This pulls our heart into the equation. Mercy mandates

forgiveness and forbearance. We love mercy when we lose our stern rigidity and celebrate the fact that none of us have received what our sins really deserve. Loving mercy helps us to refuse to obsess over a perfect house, it helps us to be flexible with our time, and it allows us to shift our priorities in order to meet needs.

To be balanced, we are to walk humbly with our God.

This is the best part of balance, because we put ourselves in a position to intimately journey with God. Instead of trying to run ahead of Him with our agenda and commitments, we simply walk with Him, in His shadow, savoring His nearness.

Do I, Jennifer, get out of balance?

Oh yes, sometimes lurching this way and that like a washing machine with a wildly imbalanced load. But most of the time, I can tell you precisely why I am out of balance. It's that nasty, five-letter word—*pride.*

Oh, I don't mean that I become all inflated and impressed with myself. (Though I know I'm capable of that too.) No, I simply mean I'm operating with the kind of pride that has little time for God and His ways because I'm busy, spinning around in my routine. That may not look arrogant to the outsider, but it's not a picture of walking humbly.

Notice that the verse doesn't say running humbly or spinning humbly. It's simply a walk. When we keep God's pace, all will be balanced.

Since we live by the Spirit, let us keep in
step with the Spirit (Galatians 5:25).

What's Percolating in Me: My Response

_____

_____

_____

_____

Spill the Beans: My Prayer

_____

_____

_____

_____

Thanks a Latte! My Praise

_____

_____

_____

_____

24

The Shelter That God Built

THE DREARY GRAY SKY ABOVE ATLANTA opened up and began to pour on my family and me as we loaded into a van with our new friends, Kurt and Lori Salierno. The dreariness of the weather was quickly displaced by the warm glow of Christian friendship and love.

We were setting out on an adventure, planning to visit one of Kurt's homeless shelters in downtown Atlanta. Several years ago, Kurt began a ministry called Church on the Street, which has now grown to minister to hundreds of men by providing food, beds, love, jobs, and Jesus.

I was anxious to see the homes that God built and meet the men who stayed there. So after dinner we piled back into the van and meandered through downtown as Kurt showed us the different places where the men slept and where they met for church.

He described to us the many reasons for homelessness and told us what to expect as we arrived at the largest shelter. I asked him how we should respond to the men we'd meet.

"Two things," he quickly answered. "Two things matter most."

He then began to explain the importance of saying their

names. "At least three times in a conversation with them, use their names. It's all they've got."

The van fell silent as he continued. "And make sure you touch them…no one ever touches them." My eyes welled up with tears as he finished his coaching.

How simple…how profound…how *Jesus*, I thought.

I too was homeless, a stranger, separated from God. He left the splendor of heaven, came to my street, and found me. Jesus Himself spoke my name and touched me. How could I do any less for His precious children—even if they happened to be dirty, disheveled, and desperate?

I have a feeling that Kurt's hands look a lot like Jesus' hands when he touches the men in his shelters. I want my hands to resemble those hands. I imagine Kurt's voice sounds a lot like His Master's voice when he acknowledges each man by name. I want my voice to resonate with the gentle tones of my Master also. And I believe the homes Kurt built reflect the heart of a divine architect who longs to bring us all into His care and shelter.

I want the relationships I build to extend this sheltering touch of Christ. So whether your footsteps take you down the streets of a big city, into the quietness of your child's bedroom, or into your local grocery store, follow Kurt's example as he follows Christ. And remember that needy people aren't always living on the streets—sometimes they drive nice cars and are well dressed.

But they too, by their very nature, are homeless and need to hear their names spoken, feel God's touch, and be drawn to His shelter.

O LORD, you are my God;
I will exalt you and praise your name,
for in perfect faithfulness
you have done marvelous things,
things planned long ago...
You have been a refuge for the poor,
a refuge for the needy in his distress,
a shelter from the storm
and a shade from the heat (Isaiah 25:1,4).

What's Percolating in Me: My Response

Spill the Beans: My Prayer

Thanks a Latte! My Praise

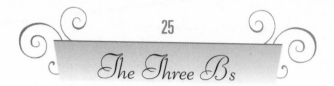

25

The Three Bs

MOTHER'S DAY GOT ME TO THINKING about what makes a great mom. I decided on three *B*s.

Now, *B* could stand for brainy, and that would be a great quality for a mom. Or it could begin the word *beautiful*, and who among us wouldn't want that adjective describing us? The *B* could also stand for buoyant or bouncy. It could begin the words *brilliant* or *bargain-bustin' babe*.

But I thought about my own mother and even though many of the above adjectives describe her, there were still three more *B*s she possesses that I hope will describe me as I grow as a mom.

The first B stands for brave.

My mother showed a quiet courage as I grew up. She confronted with gentleness, corrected with authority, and risked our friendship, valuing my future more than her own feelings. She made me do things I didn't want to do, like facing my fears, trying something again and again, apologizing when I was wrong, and cleaning the bathrooms.

It takes courage to stay with the task of motherhood with an unwavering commitment to our children when our children can create waves in our own lives.

Let's face it, motherhood takes guts. It's not for the

fainthearted; it is for girls with grit. Hebrews 10:39 should be the mantra of every brave mom: "We are not of those who shrink back."

Be brave, my fellow mom, and don't be afraid of saying no or I'm sorry. Don't shrink back from the hard stuff; our kids are worth it.

The second B stands for benevolent.

My mother displayed mercy and kindness to my brothers and me. She demonstrated the biblical truth that God does not treat us as our sins deserve (see Psalm 103:10). We often deserved far more than we got. Like the times I lied, or when my brothers and I fought...or the times I lied about fighting with my brothers!

I'm also grateful that she often applied her discipline unevenly. As I look back, it's interesting to me that it was often her kindness that led us to repentance. Her benevolence softened my heart and helped to shape my understanding of God's kindness.

Be benevolent, my fellow moms. Our kids' behavior doesn't necessarily warrant it, but God's Word recommends it. "Be kind to one another, tender-hearted, forgiving each other, just as God in Christ also has forgiven you" (Ephesians 4:32 NASB).

The third B stands for balance.

My mom knew how to strike just the right balance. She knew when to use grit and when to use grace—and when to be courageous enough to exercise justice rather than mercy. She somehow placed all the demands of her life, her kids, and her husband's ministry on the scales, and it all seemed to hang in the right proportions. Nothing fell off, nothing weighed down the rest.

I'm not sure how she did it, because *B* for balance is hard to achieve when *B* for busy is so much a part of motherhood.

Dirty dishes, dirty diapers; broken toys, broken hearts; homework, housework…these all make it hard to maintain balance at the speed of life. But strive for that balance anyway, my fellow mom—it's what our kids will remember. Be wise to recognize when to be brave and when to be benevolent, neither overreacting nor under-reacting.

Balance creates security and has a leveling effect on our children.

On January 2, 1942, a baby named Judith Lee Richbourg came into the world. On August 4, 1962 the beautiful, buoyant, Judith married Lawson E. Jolly and in just 16 months, I was born.

Now, more than 40 years later, I contemplate the three *B*s I observed in my mom, and it prompts another *B*…blessed. I do rise up and call you blessed, Mom. Thank you for living a brave, benevolent, and balanced life before me.

My friend, if you are a mom, I gently challenge you to live out the three *B*s. And if your mom is living, regardless of how flawed she may be or how many mistakes she may have made in raising you, it pleases the Lord when you honor her. In other words, you could bless God today by blessing your mom.

> *Her children stand and bless her.*
>   *Her husband praises her:*
> *"There are many virtuous and capable women*
>   *in the world,*
> *but you surpass them all!" (Proverbs 31:28–29 NLT).*

What's Percolating in Me: My Response

_____

_____

_____

_____

Spill the Beans: My Prayer

_____

_____

_____

_____

Thanks a Latte! My Praise

_____

_____

_____

_____

26

God Loves People

B<small>EFORE THE GREEN BEANS WERE SERVED</small> at the supper table, Phil removed a Scripture card from the box and read John 3:16. After he finished, he looked over at our four-year-old and asked, "Connor, what does that mean?"

Connor paused thoughtfully, and then exclaimed, "God loves people." Each of us at the table erupted in accolades of applause. "High five, Connor!" "Way to go!" "You're so smart!"

Evidently encouraged by this lavish praise, Connor said, "Dad, read another, read another!" This time, while the green beans were getting cold, Phil read Deuteronomy 8:9 (NLT): "It is a land where food is plentiful and nothing is lacking. It is a land where iron is as common as stone, and copper is abundant in the hills."

"What does that mean, Connor?" Phil asked.

Connor paused thoughtfully and then hesitantly answered, "Um, um...God loves people."

Again, we all erupted in applause. "Again, again," Connor insisted. Phil read another Scripture card. This one featured a verse in 1 Peter about how we should each serve God with the strength He gives us. As soon as Phil finished the reading, Connor yelled, "I know what it means, I know what it means... it means GOD LOVES PEOPLE!"

We could hardly contain our collective chuckles as we clapped for his earnest attempt. You see, what we thought was certain genius after John 3:16 simply turned out to be more like a Pavlovian response to positive reinforcement. That's okay though because Connor actually was correct about each verse.

Whether the verse we read was about God's faithfulness or how He strengthens us to serve, the core of each verse is the truth that God does indeed love people. He loves strong people, weak people, four-year-old people, people who succeed, and people who struggle. He loves people who wear uniforms and fight in foreign lands, and He loves people who pray for their safe return. He loves the wise and the foolish, the leader and the follower. And, my friend, He loves you.

Every word in His Book reveals the love of a Father that is unconditional and boundless. Again, my child has become my teacher, and I learn again the purpose of this holy Book I cherish. Its purpose is to reveal how deep and broad is the love of God for people.

His Word speaks the language of love to each heart—and I'm so grateful He sent me a love letter that reassures me of His love. So read it, learn it, and repeat it often, for God really does long for people to know how much He loves them.

I have loved you with an
everlasting love (Jeremiah 31:3).

◗ What's Percolating in Me: My Response

_____

_____

_____

_____

◗ Spill the Beans: My Prayer

_____

_____

_____

_____

◗ Thanks a Latte! My Praise

_____

_____

_____

_____

27

Trust His Heart

PART OF THE BEDTIME ROUTINE around my house is to practice memory verses with Connor. Our practice involves singing along with Scripture on cassette as we snuggle under the covers.

On one particularly hectic week, bedtimes were a little later than usual, and we didn't get to practice as much as we needed. That meant I brought the Fisher-Price tape player to the dinner table, and we crammed in a practice session over pizza before we left for church. The children's voices on the tape started to serenade us with a verse from Ephesians, "Children, obey your parents in the Lord, for this is right."

Connor listened with great concentration and then observed, "Mom, that must be your favorite verse."

My oldest son, Clayton, burst into laughter and quipped, "Oh, Connor if you only knew. That's *every* parent's favorite verse." I laughed too and reminded the boys that it wouldn't have to be my favorite verse if it became *their* favorite verse.

Actually, I do have great appreciation for the obedience admonition in Ephesians, but it isn't my favorite verse. My favorite verse seems to change with the seasons of my life.

I remember vividly the season when 1 Thessalonians 5:18 was at the top of my list. I was in my mid-twenties, trying to adjust to my disability and seeking to learn the discipline of a thankful heart. I was pretty good at being thankful for all the easy, good, and blessed moments of life. It was the difficult, hard, and seemingly unfair things that challenged my gratitude quotient.

I began to quote "give thanks in all circumstances" often. I have found over the years that the practice has now become a privilege. What began as a duty and discipline has now become a delight.

We have plenty of opportunities to practice gratefulness in "all circumstances" because many circumstances can be exceedingly difficult to be grateful for—like illness, betrayal, conflict, and disappointment. Blind eyes have enabled me to see that I can be thankful in all things when I realize that God is in charge of all things.

Who am I to determine what is a good thing or blessing from the hand of God? I've found that some of the blessings He leaves on our doorstep are wrapped in some pretty rough paper. Some gifts are hard to recognize because they don't look anything like what we were hoping for. But as someone has well said, "God is too wise to be mistaken; God is too wise to be unkind. When you can't trace His hand, that's when you must learn to trust His heart."

I can always be thankful to God for His kind heart and unwavering character. And so can you. If we are truly to be thankful in all things, it will happen only if we are focused on the heart of God. His ways may confuse us for the moment, but knowing His heart always calms us.

If we base our gratitude on the God who gives and allows only good and perfect gifts, we will explode with thankfulness. He is in charge of all things, so be thankful in all today.

*Give thanks in all circumstances, for this is God's
will for you in Christ Jesus (1 Thessalonians 5:18).*

🫘 What's Percolating in Me: My Response

_____

_____

_____

_____

🫘 Spill the Beans: My Prayer

_____

_____

_____

_____

🫘 Thanks a Latte! My Praise

_____

_____

_____

_____

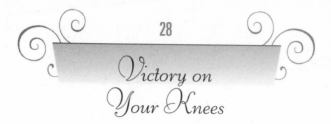

28

Victory on Your Knees

IN JUNE OF 2002, we all learned of the news that the Philippine army had made an attempt to rescue Martin and Gracia Burnham. The Burnhams were New Tribes Missionaries who had been held hostage by Muslim extremists for more than a year, but their struggle ended with the fateful rescue attempt.

Gracia survived a gunshot wound, but her husband, Martin, did not. Details were unclear as to how and why he received a fatal bullet. What is clear, however, is that he was released from captivity…and went home to heaven. His tragedy became his triumph. Gracia, however, is now home in America with her children.

She is the reason I write these words. She is the reason I have prayed for the last many months. Although I have never met her, she has become my sister.

When the news of their captivity first broke, I too was captivated. Drawn to their story, I felt compelled to pray and carry their burden in a way beyond anything I had experienced before. My heart was immediately knit to Gracia's. But somehow, even though her captivity has ended, my burden has not lifted. Gracia came home alone. Her tragedy has not yet become a triumph, for she now has to learn how to live without her beloved husband and struggle to find her new place in this world.

The pages of her life have contained high drama and deep sorrow, but she is not unlike you and me. She is an example of what exists all around us. There are sisters in bondage, struggling to experience freedom. There are sisters left alone in the world, desperately trying to find their place. Yet as with Gracia, their triumph will come. It may be slow and arduous, but it will come.

I am committed to be a part of Gracia's victory through my prayer. It was not a coincidence that the news of their kidnapping sunk so deeply into my heart, and so I will continue to allow the cords of empathy that God has wrapped around my heart to keep me on my knees for Gracia Burnham.

Always be sensitive to the Spirit's tug when He lays a sister's burden on your heart. You don't have to know her to love her. God may be calling you to be part of her victory as you intercede on her behalf. You will find that as you stand in the gap for others, you too receive a victory. It's a victory over self. It's the victory that comes from enlarging your heart and broadening your view.

And so, my sisters, pray. Someone may experience victory because you are on your knees.

> *But thanks be to God! He gives us the*
> *victory through our Lord Jesus Christ*
> *(1 Corinthians 15:57).*

What's Percolating in Me: My Response

Spill the Beans: My Prayer

Thanks a Latte! My Praise

29

Keep Shining

DURING SUMMER VACATION before Clayton started middle school and Connor started preschool, my husband, Phil, took a short weekend trip for work. The boys and I were home alone. We had a fun time together with water guns, pizza, and Popsicles. When bedtime arrived, I carefully locked all the doors, shut the blinds, and turned on the porch light.

I put Connor to bed and let our oldest son, Clayton, stay up late with me. We watched videos and then camped out on my bedroom floor in sleeping bags. By 11:30, lights were out and we were sleepy. Just as we began to nod off, my front door shook with a loud thump. The door knocker rattled, and I panicked.

Clayton shot up from his sleeping bag. "Mom, what was that?"

I tried to act nonchalant while my heart raced. "Oh," I said, "It was probably just the cat. You know how clumsy he is. I think he slid across the tile and slammed into the door."

Remarkably, Clayton laughed and settled back down. I, of course, started a marathon of private and panicked praying. *What was that?* I wondered. *There's no way I'm going to check.* And then remarkably, I settled down and fell asleep.

The next morning, I opened the front door with our youngest son, Connor, to retrieve the newspaper. "Yuck, Mommy!"

he exclaimed. "There's eggs all over the front porch!" No sooner had he said this than the pungent smell of rotten eggs wafted in. The mystery was solved.

I had blamed the bang and thump on the clumsy cat, but it was really the result of the incredible edible egg—albeit past its prime. I aroused Clayton to help me survey the damage, and cleanup began. He quickly checked out the other neighbors' porches for yolks and shells, but they were clean.

Was the attack personal? I wondered. *Why our porch and no one else's?* Then it dawned on me as we scrubbed away the eggy evidence.

"It was the light," I told Clayton. None of our neighbors had their porch lights on the night before, and we did. Our light made us a target.

Well, my friend, guess what? Your light makes you a target too. When you shine brightly for Christ, your light makes you really obvious—and the enemy stands poised for an attack.

Consider it a compliment and an honor when the enemy throws his darts your direction. Your light threatens his darkness. Don't be intimidated by his slimy schemes. He may rattle you, but he can't overcome you. The apostle John reminds us that He who lives in us is greater than he who lives in the world. The light of Christ in you will always prevail over darkness.

Keep shining for Jesus.

Let your light shine before men, that they may see your good deeds and praise your Father in heaven (Matthew 5:16).

What's Percolating in Me: My Response

_____

_____

_____

_____

Spill the Beans: My Prayer

_____

_____

_____

_____

Thanks a Latte! My Praise

_____

_____

_____

_____

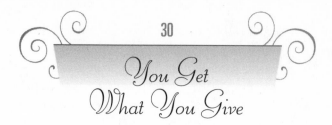

30

You Get
What You Give

HAVE YOU EVER FELT LIKE GIVING UP OR GIVING IN? I sure have. There have been mornings when I arise early, get the boys ready for school, kiss everyone goodbye…and then go back and crawl into bed.

Why? Because some days I just want to give up. The pressures seem too great, the burdens feel too heavy, and the light at the end of the tunnel is too dim and distant.

We all feel like giving up from time to time. We long for the battle to end, and it appears that waving a white flag and crying "surrender" would create an immediate cease-fire.

At other times, I feel as if I can no longer suppress the urge to give in. It would be much easier to just get mad, become bitter, and harbor resentment. After all, life didn't turn out the way I expected.

Sometimes blindness peels back every layer of my resistance and scrapes the surface of my soul. I know the apostle Paul tells us to rejoice always, but sometimes I'd just like to throw a pity party and intentionally leave Paul off the guest list. Sometimes we all feel worn thin and wonder if the tension might be relieved a little if we would could take a vacation from our spiritual disciplines and just give in to our feelings.

The problem, however, with giving up or giving in is that we get what we give. Galatians 6:7 says that "a man reaps what he sows." That means that if I choose to give up, I will simply get defeat in return. If I choose to give in, I will surely receive the fruits of a self-life, including such unsavory items as bitterness and anger. But if on those dark days I deliberately choose to exercise my faith and give praise and thanks rather than giving up and giving in...well, my sisters, then I receive the matchless benefits of being in God's will and experiencing His presence.

First Thessalonians 5:18 tells us that when we give thanks, we are participating in the will of God. When we find ourselves in His will, we are in the prime posture to receive. When we choose to give praise, we experience the very presence of God in our midst. God Himself inhabits the praises of His people. If we give praise, we receive His presence. And in His presence is fullness of joy.

Be encouraged, my friend. To give up and give in might seem easier, but what you will get when you give praise and give thanks far outweighs the burden you feel right now.

So keep your shoes on and walk by faith. Make those feelings of weariness, the urges to give up, and the temptations to give in bow to your faith. Walk on even when you're weary and fight even when you're frail. Even if you have only a mustard-seed-sized faith, use it to give thanks and give praise. When you do, you will see it grow, for what you get is a result of what you give.

Let us not become weary in doing good,
for at the proper time we will reap a harvest
if we do not give up (Galatians 6:9).

What's Percolating in Me: My Response

_____

_____

_____

Spill the Beans: My Prayer

_____

_____

_____

Thanks a Latte! My Praise

_____

_____

_____

31

Oh, What Love!

THE FIRST DAY CONNOR WENT TO KINDERGARTEN, I meticulously packed his lunch. A squeezable juice box, a custom-crafted sandwich, and baby carrots accompanied my little guy into the big world of elementary school. His lunchbox was not complete, though, until I placed a napkin bearing a handwritten "I love you" deep inside.

I followed this loving routine each morning. But at the end of the week, Connor came home with a request.

"Mom," he asked, "do you have to write on my napkins?" He took a deep breath and announced, "I just don't want you to write on them because when I'm done, I feel like I'm throwing your love away!"

"Oh, Connor," I exclaimed, flinging my arms around his little frame, "just because you throw away your napkin doesn't mean you throw my love away!"

He giggled in relief—and confessed he didn't really use napkins anyway.

I was struck by Connor's sensitive heart, and it made me examine my own. Do I carelessly throw away God's love for me? Do I casually dismiss the small and big ways God expresses His love to me?

Do you? We all do sometimes, just as the wayward Israelites did in Hosea's day.

Hosea was a young preacher at a time when religious folks didn't want to hear his message. The Jews were more interested in idolatry than worshipping the Lord. They were like the hymn writer who penned, "Prone to wander…prone to leave the God I love."

One day God told Hosea his bachelor days were up. The problem with the wedding announcement was that it came accompanied with a dreadful prophecy. God was going to use Hosea's marriage as a graphic picture of the nation's infidelity to their Lord. Here's the way it reads in the Living Bible:

> The Lord said to Hosea, "Go and marry a girl who is a prostitute, so that some of her children will be born to you from other men. This will illustrate the way my people have been untrue to me, committing open adultery against me by worshiping other gods" (Hosea 1:2 TLB).

How do you think Hosea must have felt? Do you think he fully believed what God predicted would really happen? He knew of Gomer. Would the marriage turn out as tragic as the Lord's words seemed to imply? Obediently, Hosea pursued, courted, won, and married her. I like to think that maybe the early years of their marriage held some happiness for the couple. Did they enjoy late-night talks, stolen kisses in the courtyard, and holding hands as they drifted off to sleep?

Maybe…and maybe not.

But what we do know is that after the children came along, whatever marriage dreams Hosea and Gomer might have enjoyed in the early days warped into a nightmare. The Bible doesn't say when or how. All we know is that Hosea began to hear rumors. His heart began to break. His beloved Gomer was going off with other men. Then he came home one night to find the kids home alone and a note on the table announcing she was gone. Hosea, a brokenhearted father, a betrayed husband, and a bewildered preacher, must have felt as if his heart would never recover.

The final blow? Gomer's wanderings had led her into prostitution and slavery. In that moment of gut-wrenching agony, God tells His servant to go buy her back—to redeem her.

Who could have blamed the prophet if he had cried out to God, "She's thrown my love away! Why should I have to buy back what's already mine?"

Nevertheless, Hosea was an obedient man, and the Lord's instructions were clear: "Go, show your love to your wife again, though she is loved by another and is an adulteress. Love her as the Lord loves the Israelites, though they turn to other gods" (Hosea 3:1).

Can you imagine the lonely, heartbroken prophet walking up to a town square and seeing the woman he loved, the mother of his children, standing in front of the crowd, barely clothed, being auctioned off to the highest bidder?

Here is how the Living Bible paraphrases that devastating moment: "So I bought her back from her slavery for a couple of dollars and eight bushels of barley" (Hosea 3:2).

The auctioneer's hammer fell as he pronounced, "Sold!"

Can you imagine her glancing up to see who her new master would be—and seeing Hosea? Do you think her eyes filled with tears? Hosea walked his wife off the slave block, covered her with his cloak and whispered in her ear, "You are to live with me many days; you must not be a prostitute or be intimate with any man, and I will live with you" (Hosea 3:3).

Hosea was a faithful husband; Gomer was an unfaithful wife.

God is the faithful lover of our souls. We are often faithless, prone to wander. God is a covenant keeper. We are covenant breakers.

Hosea and Gomer's story is the story of God and Israel. But it's also *our* story. When we, like Gomer, were enslaved, God bought us back. When we, by our very nature, threw God's love away, He redeemed us. When Hosea bought Gomer back, He did so with 15 shekels of silver and some barley—the cost of an ordinary slave. When God redeemed us, however, He paid the highest price in the universe: the lifeblood of His own precious Son (1 Peter 1:18-19).

Gomer didn't deserve to be redeemed. Her behavior did not merit such mercy. Israel did not deserve God's faithful betrothal. Their unfaithfulness did not merit such mercy. Nor do you and I! We don't deserve salvation; our sin doesn't merit such mercy.

Why did God redeem you? Why did Jesus pay the ultimate price for your purchase? Why does God continue to give His unconditional love to a people who continually throw it away? Not because we deserve it, but because mercy demands it. Aren't you glad God doesn't treat us as our sin deserves?

My friend, do you carelessly throw away God's love?

God has written on your very life the words *I LOVE YOU.* He values you so much that He enters into covenant with you, redeems you, and remains faithful to you. Oh, what love!

He does not treat us as our sins deserve
or repay us according to our iniquities.
For as high as the heavens are above the earth,
so great is his love for those who fear him
(Psalm 103:10–11).

❧ What's Percolating in Me: My Response

_____

_____

_____

❧ Spill the Beans: My Prayer

_____

_____

_____

❧ Thanks a Latte! My Praise

_____

_____

_____

32

A Better Plan B

CONNOR ALWAYS ADDS FLAIR TO the Rothschild family doings.

As I made dinner one evening, he decided that he should make dessert to go along with dinner. And so with his own recipe to guide him, my little kindergarten chef began fashioning mounds of Play-Doh into scoops of ice cream.

As I stirred the rice, he got up from the table and removed a little sherbet dish from the cupboard. As I placed the bread in the oven, Connor meticulously placed his ice cream scoops into the delicate dish.

"Strawberry and vanilla," I heard him exclaim as his little fingers shaped a tiny cherry for the top.

Then, just as quickly as ice cream melts on a hot July afternoon, his enthusiasm melted away.

"What's wrong?" I asked.

"Its falling apart!" he moaned. "My cherry won't stick. My vanilla is getting smashed into my strawberry. It doesn't look good anymore."

I left the stove to survey the culinary disaster that was now all over the table. Connor was right. His masterpiece was mushy, and his statuesque sundae had collapsed. His dessert had wilted, and so had his spirit.

"Well, Connor, I guess you need a plan B."

He sighed deeply, and then announced, "Okay, I have a plan B."

"Well, what is it?"

"Quit!" he huffed. "My plan A was to do it right. My plan B is to quit." He followed that proclamation with a groan: "Aaarrgh!"

I wanted to burst into laughter over his blunt honesty, but I held my giggle. Instead, I coaxed him to make quitting his plan Z. That meant he had 24 other options to try before he threw in the towel. And so a toothpick nicely wedged between vanilla and strawberry became the new plan B. His faux ice cream creation was lifted, and so was his spirit.

Connor's honest response echoed how we all feel from time to time. We may not express it with an "argh," but deep down, when things aren't turning out as we'd hoped, when they seem to be falling apart, we too would like to execute plan B and quit.

Abraham must have believed plan B was a better idea as he trudged up Mount Moriah. Elijah must have wished for a plan B as he ran from Jezebel. Hosea must have longed for a plan B as he headed toward the slave market to buy back Gomer. They felt it, I've felt it, you've felt it. But quitting isn't a plan, it's a cop-out!

That's why we need to take the advice of the apostle James and "consider it pure joy." Why? Because we know that the testing of our faith leads to a better plan B—perseverance.

Oh, my sisters, if your dreams have gotten smashed, if your ideas haven't worked out as you hoped, don't give up. Let plan B unfold as you persevere. If you let perseverance have its perfect work in you, you will become mature, lacking nothing.

Perseverance is always a better plan B. It will lift your spirit and lead you to maturity. Be encouraged today, and don't give up. And if you really feel like you need to quit...procrastinate!

> *Consider it pure joy, my brothers, whenever you face trials of many kinds, because you know that the testing of your faith develops perseverance. Perseverance must finish its work so that you may be mature and complete, not lacking anything (James 1:2-3).*

🫘 What's Percolating in Me: My Response

_____

_____

🫘 Spill the Beans: My Prayer

_____

_____

🫘 Thanks a Latte! My Praise

_____

_____

33

Three-Star Boldness

ONE TUESDAY IN JANUARY, Connor was asked by his friend Jacob, "Where are your mom and dad?" With customary confidence and typical first-grade logic, Connor responded, "They are with my Uncle David, Aunt Carrie, and George Washington in State of Union."

He was partly right. Tuesday night, January 31, Phil and I had the once-in-a-lifetime privilege of attending the State of the Union address presented by President George W. Bush. Before the speech, we were invited to dinner with the congressman for whom my brother David worked at the time.

We met at the Capitol Hill Club for a lovely dinner with the congressman, his wife, and several Navy admirals and Bethesda Naval Hospital doctors.

Just before we went into the dining room, David whispered to me that our seats for the annual address were located near the First Lady. It was all I could do to contain my excitement. As we stood in the lobby waiting for our table, with senators and congressmen passing by, I wanted to start screaming, "Phil and I are going to the State of the Union, and I am sitting near Laura Bush!"

Reasonably certain that none of the seasoned Washington professionals would share or understand my enthusiasm, I mustered all the self-control I could and remained quietly composed—though every nerve in my body was shaking with excitement.

I could not believe we were about to sit in the gallery for such a historic occasion. To think that in 1913, Woodrow Wilson stood in that very hall and addressed both houses of congress in person after 112 years of the annual message being presented only in writing. And now, somehow, little Jennifer Rothschild was about to experience such an event firsthand.

As I waited to be seated for dinner, I thought about that hallowed hall we were about to enter. It was the very hall where Calvin Coolidge's 1923 speech was first broadcast on radio. And where Harry Truman's 1947 message was actually seen by the nation, the first State of the Union message to be televised. But to my surprise, I was just as awestruck by what happened at dinner prior to the president's address.

We were seated by a very distinguished and intelligent admiral. After interesting and casual conversation over dinner, our exchange took on a sweeter and more intimate flavor as dessert was served. Amid the fragrance of fine coffee and crème brûlée, he began to talk about the genuine faith of President Bush he witnessed when escorting him to see the many war heroes at Bethesda. Without prompting, the admiral mentioned the importance of faith, and then he announced, "My faith is in the Lord Jesus Christ."

"Mine too," I chimed. "Mine too," Phil added with brotherly love.

Suddenly I felt an unexpected thrill. Here was an admiral, a man responsible for all of Navy medicine, unashamed to announce his loyalty to his Savior—and this was before he knew much about me or Phil.

Sitting across from that bold warrior of Christ made me rethink the history and heroes that were filling my thoughts on such a special night.

It's true, to be a part of such an event as the State of the Union Address was nothing to take lightly. But to be face-to-face with a hero of the faith who wore three earthly stars on his uniform but wore the scars of His Savior on his heart—that was something that impacted me deeply.

Yes, for a political junkie like me, the speech was incredible to hear in person. The atmosphere in the gallery that night was electric. But what happened in my heart during dessert made an indelible impact that is now a part of *my* history, and it will inspire me to make that kind of boldness part of my posterity as well.

Oh, that you and I would be that kind of hero. That you and I with boldness would proclaim our allegiance to Christ. Regardless of the setting we find ourselves in, regardless of the company we are with, let us hold fast to our faith and make it known.

> *Therefore, since we have such a hope,*
> *we are very bold (2 Corinthians 3:12).*

What's Percolating in Me: My Response

_____

_____

Spill the Beans: My Prayer

_____

_____

Thanks a Latte! My Praise

_____

_____

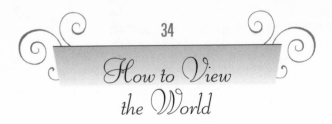

34

How to View the World

ONCE UPON A FUTON, Connor confidently announced to me, "Mom, I want to be an astronaut."

He was five years old at the time and about to start kindergarten, so I figured he'd thought long and hard about this decision.

"So why do you want to be an astronaut, Connor?"

"Well," he observed, "astronauts get to walk on the moon and they can see the world better than anyone else."

"That's interesting," I replied. "How can you see the world so well from up there?"

"The world is easier to see," he explained, "when you're not in it."

My little space traveler made a poignant observation that his earthbound mom needed to recognize. It is hard to see the world clearly when you're in the midst of its routines. When we heavenly citizens spend too much time taking in the messages of the world, we become desensitized. We recognize less and less how foreign it really is to our true culture.

Sometimes we just need to blast off, get a renewed heavenly perspective and look back at our planet and its ways through the lens of Scripture. Then we'll see it all more clearly.

As sojourners, our customs are not those of this world; they're kingdom customs.

When the world tells us to keep a big chip on our shoulders and make our violators pay dearly, our custom is forgiveness (Matthew 6:14; Luke 17:3-4).

When the world tells us to look out for number one and remember that charity begins at home, our custom is sacrificial compassion (Ephesians 4:32; Colossians 3:12).

When the world tells us to get all we can, to buy now and pay later, our custom is wide-open generosity (Matthew 5:41-42).

When the world tells us to "just do it," our custom is self-discipline (2 Peter 1:5-8).

When the world says you can have it your way, our custom is altruism and humility (Philippians 2:3).

When the world claims that it is the real thing, our custom is to fix our eyes on unseen realities (2 Corinthians 4:18).

When the world tells us to say, "I'm worth it," our custom is to say, "He is worthy" (Revelation 4:11).

We believers are called to be in the world, yet we are equally admonished to avoid allowing the world to squeeze us into its mold.

When we soar on the wings of truth, when we're carried by the winds of grace, then we can see our world and our role in it far more clearly.

> *Don't become so well-adjusted to your culture that you fit into it without even thinking. Instead, fix your attention on God. You'll be changed from the inside out. Readily recognize what he wants from*

you, and quickly respond to it. Unlike the culture around you, always dragging you down to its level of immaturity, God brings the best out of you, develops well-formed maturity in you (Romans 12:2 MSG).

❧

What's Percolating in Me: My Response

_____

_____

_____

Spill the Beans: My Prayer

_____

_____

_____

Thanks a Latte! My Praise

_____

_____

_____

35

Nobody Clapped

MY LITTLE CONNOR IS LEARNING A LOT MORE in kindergarten than just how to write his name, stand still in line, and raise his hand in class. He's also learning how to handle discouragement.

When Connor disembarked from his yellow school bus after school, he carried much more than a backpack full of painted construction paper and pencil-scratched worksheets. He also carried a burden of disappointment all the way home from Mrs. Setzer's classroom. He had picked up this heavy and unfamiliar baggage at show-and-tell earlier that day.

Without even seeing his cute face, I knew that all was not well just by the sound of his voice. I called out from the front porch, "Hi, Connor."

"Hi, Mom."

"What's wrong?"

His small voice broke. "Mom, nobody clapped."

"What do you mean?"

"At show-and-tell, nobody clapped for me." His voice rose with conviction as he indignantly announced, "They all clapped for Devin, but nobody clapped for *me!*"

Connor told me that the class had never clapped during show-and-tell before today, but something about Devin's display had prompted the unusual kindergarten ovation.

"Well," I consoled, "maybe it's because Devin made the picture all by himself, and your classmates were simply being encouraging."

I heard a big sigh. "Mom, I need en-touragement too."

Now it was time for mom to bind up the emotional wounds. "Connor," I said, "people aren't always going to clap—even when we do something great. Sometimes people applaud for others and not for us. I know it feels good when we hear clapping, but when you don't hear people applaud, it's easier to hear God's applause."

That caught his attention. "God claps?"

"Yes," I continued. "We can't hear God clapping with our ears, but we hear it with our hearts."

I'm not sure he really understood the point, but I pray that someday he will. There certainly will be many times in life when we don't receive the acknowledgment or praise we feel we need or deserve. Let's face it—sometimes we all crave an "Atta boy!" or "Atta girl!" But being so focused on the praise of men may leave us deflated and discouraged. It can distract us from hearing the one who delights to applaud our progress as we walk by faith and run the race with endurance.

The apostle Paul wrote, "Am I now trying to win the approval of men, or of God? Or am I trying to please men? If I were still trying to please men, I would not be a servant of Christ" (Galatians 1:10).

His applause may be quiet and subtle. You may hear it as you read His Word or receive a touch from a sister in Christ. It can be heard in lonely silence and in loud crowds. You can sense it as you draw near to Him and as you flee from sin. You hear its faint echo as you obey even when no one here on earth is watching.

Yes, God sees, God knows, God claps. There is enough revealed about our God through the pages of Scripture to suggest that if clapping occurs in heaven, God is applauding for you. He is like the faithful father in the story Jesus told about the prodigal son in Luke 15. It shows that our God is ready to run to a wayward child and celebrate with an outrageous party on his homecoming.

Surely the Father claps. Surely the child is encouraged.

Frankly, the reason we don't hear the applause of heaven is probably that we're not listening for it. Our ears are so fixed on the temporary accolades of men that we are deaf to the eternal applause of our Father God.

The applause of men fades; the applause of our God is forever. Listen for it, and you will certainly hear it.

And by the way, His applause isn't based on what you do. It's based on who, or shall I say, *whose,* you are.

> *The LORD your God is in your midst,*
> *A victorious warrior.*
> *He will exult over you with joy,*
> *He will be quiet in His love,*
> *He will rejoice over you with shouts of joy*
> *(Zephaniah 3:17 NASB).*

What's Percolating in Me: My Response

_____

_____

_____

_____

Spill the Beans: My Prayer

_____

_____

_____

_____

Thanks a Latte! My Praise

_____

_____

_____

_____

36

A New
Point of View

READING PSALM 73 IS LIKE READING SOMEONE'S BLOG. Asaph, the troubled psalmist, is bluntly candid about his struggle with the prosperity of the wicked. To him, the people of God seemed to be struggling with affliction while those who couldn't care less about God were swimming in cream. His fellow believers were pressured while the blasphemers were cashing in on the good life. So Asaph journaled his feelings—what was percolating in him—writing honestly about how hard it was to reconcile the apparent inequities.

At one point, almost overwhelmed with the unfairness of life, he admitted he was on the cliff-edge of losing his faith: "As for me, I came *so* close to the edge of the cliff! My feet were slipping and I was almost gone. For I was envious of the prosperity of the proud and wicked (Psalm 73:2-3 TLB).

We know how he felt, don't we? When we see godly people suffer and godless people soar, we too can rightly become confused and frustrated. About 2500 years have passed since Asaph penned those words, but nothing has really changed. You or I could just as easily write them today. It seems sometimes like Billy Joel had it right when he wrote, "Only the Good Die Young."

If I were Asaph, I would have vented and complained about the frustrating unfairness. Believe me, just traveling in airports these days challenges me in this area.

But that's *not* what Asaph did. He didn't rant and rave to anyone who would listen. He kept his mouth shut.

Eugene Peterson paraphrases Asaph's words like this: "If I'd have given in and talked like this, I would have betrayed your dear children" (Psalm 73:15 MSG).

Asaph was victorious in his struggle because he kept a respect for God and His people. And his profound respect led to a profound restraint. He noted candidly that "my feet had almost slipped; I had nearly lost my foothold" (verse 2).

But guess what? *Neither* happened.

He may have lost his balance for a moment, may have felt a touch of spiritual vertigo, but he didn't fall, and he didn't do anything he had to regret later.

Notice that he mentioned nothing about having respect for the wicked or their behavior, but out of respect for God and in an effort to keep God's people from stumbling, he refrained from speaking with ill will.

How wise to use restraint and not share each thought we have. I've heard it said, "Think twice, speak once." In doing so, the second thought may correct or bring truth to the first thought. Of course, the best-case scenario is to not think ill thoughts in the first place, but it's much worse to speak them and infect the listener.

Just like the psalmist, we control our words because we respect God and His people. We don't want our words to be a stumbling block.

But let's be honest here. We can respect and refrain, biting our tongue and biding our time, but sometimes we need a whole new perspective. A fresh way of looking at things.

That's eventually the conclusion Asaph came to. When he just couldn't resolve his quandary with the whole thing, he got a new point of view.

He went on to say, "When I tried to understand all this, it was oppressive to me till I entered the sanctuary of God; then I understood" (Psalm 73:16-17). As long as he tried to squeeze meaning out of his circumstances in the strength of his own human brain, he was in absolute turmoil. But then he made the best decision he could have made.

He went into the sanctuary. In the presence of the living God, and in that encounter with the Holy One, all of those troubling questions didn't seem so oppressive any more.

Only in the light of divine revelation and in the light of His presence is our searching settled. The sanctuary is the place where our frustrations fade. In fact, in light of God's grace and mercy, our ponderings often give way to praise.

I *want* that, don't you? I want my wonderings and my wanderings to turn into worship. I want to fix my gaze on the light in the sanctuary rather than the darkness of my own heart and the hearts of others. Not everything can be reconciled in our minds, but in everything we can still reverence God in our hearts, and *that* makes all the difference.

So when you are faced with the apparent unfairness of life, when the righteous seem to struggle while the unrighteous succeed, use wise restraint and go to the sanctuary to gain a better perspective.

May your ponderings lead you to praise.

> *With Your counsel You will guide me,*
> *And afterward receive me to glory.*
> *Whom have I in heaven but You?*
> *And besides You, I desire nothing on earth.*
> *My flesh and my heart may fail,*
> *But God is the strength of my heart and my portion*
> *forever (Psalm 73:24-26 NASB).*

🫘 What's Percolating in Me: My Response

_____

_____

🫘 Spill the Beans: My Prayer

_____

_____

🫘 Thanks a Latte! My Praise

_____

_____

37

Not Enough Time

CONNOR AND HIS FELLOW FIRST GRADERS had been instructed to bring show-and-tell items to school shortly after Christmas. His teacher sent home specific instructions about how they were to present their special items. The rules included admonishments like these: Choose an item that is meaningful to you and practice explaining its significance to your family so you'll be prepared to share with your classmates. Be prepared to answer questions, and keep your explanations to a five-minute maximum.

So with such a lofty assignment, Connor sat on his bedroom floor surrounded with toys, books, trophies, and pictures. He sighed heavily as he rifled through the potential show-and-tell fodder and then called me to his room to share his dilemma.

"Mom, I can't decide what to bring. My stuff isn't as good as Ana Lee's. She got to bring Elvis, her dog."

Somehow, to his seven-year-old worldview, old family pictures and once-favored toys paled in comparison to a real, live, furry dog. I understood his quandary, so I offered what I thought was a sensational solution: "Connor, you can take Clayton! I bet no one else brings a teenage brother."

Without even a hint of contemplation, Connor flatly responded, "There's not enough time to explain him."

I burst out in laughter at the sage insight from such young

lips. But he's more correct than he can even imagine. Some mysteries of life and faith simply cannot be explained. Time just won't allow it.

Part of being human means that for a season, we are wedded to time and space. We are housed in our earthly bodies and subject to limitations, and one of them is time. Time represents our restricted capacity—it shows that we are at the mercy of our planet and our own humanity.

God instituted time in creation. Morning and evening made each day. He created time for us, but not us for time. At least not ultimately. In the final analysis, we were made for eternity.

You've heard the well-worn expressions...

> "I don't have enough time."
> "I ran out of time."
> "My, how time flies."
> "Time caught up with me."

These expressions demonstrate our astonishment at the passage of time. The boundaries set by each tick of the clock are counterintuitive to us. They run contrary to our spiritual nature.

Just recently, tears trickled down my cheeks at a funeral for James, a college student. Did I cry over the loss of our precious friend? Of course I did. But each tear I wept was also from an awareness of the general injustice of time and our short stays on this planet.

We were not made to die. We were created for eternity. The book of Ecclesiastes tells us that God has placed that awareness deep in man's inmost being.

> He has also set eternity in the hearts of men; yet
> they cannot fathom what God has done from
> beginning to end (Ecclesiastes 3:11).

The mourning that sweeps over us each time we feel the sting of death represents our chafing against the constraints of time.

George Washington Carver, who began his life as a slave and ended it as a horticulturalist, chemist, and educator, once said, "I said to God, 'God, tell me the mystery of the universe.' But God answered, 'That knowledge is for Me alone.' So, I said, 'God, tell me the mystery of the peanut.' Then God said, 'Well, George, that's more nearly your size.'"

Huge eternal mysteries are not solvable in our peanut-size time and space. But the very fact that we grapple with such questions, longing for understanding and explanation, reflects that we were not made for time and space—we were made for eternity.

Our ambivalent relationship with time exposes a capacity and deep longing within us for that which is eternal. Time limits us, but it also reminds us that we were not made for time. So if you struggle with unanswered questions, don't let the mystery weigh you down and make you weary. Instead, let it awaken in you the reassuring truth that you are timeless.

> *It is done. I am the Alpha and the Omega, the*
> *Beginning and the End. To him who is thirsty I*
> *will give to drink without cost from the spring of the*
> *water of life (Revelation 20:6).*

What's Percolating in Me: My Response

_____

_____

_____

_____

Spill the Beans: My Prayer

_____

_____

_____

_____

Thanks a Latte! My Praise

_____

_____

_____

_____

38

Learning Optimism

CONNOR CAME HOME FROM SCHOOL downcast, gloomily admitting, "I got in trouble today." He went on to tell me that he had been caught "fake talking," as he put it.

Fake talking?

Apparently, the infraction came down like this. When the cafeteria monitor told the kids to have a moment of silence, he turned to his friend and proceeded to shake his head and silently move if his mouth as if he were having a conversation. Fake talk. I told him that even though he hadn't been verbal, he was still pushing the boundaries, and it was no wonder he got noticed.

His real punishment for the fake crime was to sit on the cafeteria stage the next day and eat lunch by himself. He was distraught at that prospect, full of dread and totally hopeless about the future of his elementary career.

I offered the usual consolations. "It will be okay...This isn't the worst thing that's ever happened...In five years, you won't even remember it." And for the finale, I said, "Connor, this one thing won't ruin your life."

"I know that one thing won't ruin your life," he sighed. "But *two* might. And now I'm halfway there!"

Little Connor needed some big encouragement. He needed to turn his pessimism into optimism.

Have you ever felt that way, as if you were just one mistake away from failure, one choice away from blowing it?

Ahh...the Land of Halfway There. That gray, twilight place where you can turn toward optimism or pessimism. Winston Churchill once said, "The pessimist sees difficulty in every opportunity. The optimist sees the opportunity in every difficulty."

Optimism isn't a feeling we feel; it's a choice we make. In fact, Martin E.P. Seligman, author of *Learned Optimism*, said, "Optimism is a learned skill. Once learned, it increases achievement at work and improves physical health."

For believers, optimism and hope are more than simple learned skills. They are our birthright. The wise psalmist affirmed the reason for optimism and hope as he spoke to his soul: "Why are you downcast, O my soul...hope in God" (Psalm 42:5).

Hope is putting faith to work when giving up would be easier. We all feel despair at times, and we can all grow in optimism as we tell our souls to not give in to that despair but rather to choose hope. Whatever you are going through today, don't choose to believe the worst; believe God. Choose to be hopeful, and instead of focusing on the fact that you are "halfway there," focus on the truth that you have come a long way. See your difficulty as an opportunity to train your soul to be optimistic.

So, my friend, be joyful in hope (Romans 12:12). It holds the seeds of faith and love (Colossians 1:5). It is the foundation for faith and knowledge (Titus 1:2). Hope is your calling (Ephesians 1:18); hope is alive (1 Peter 1:3); hope is a gift from God (Jeremiah 29:11); hope is Christ in you (Colossians 1:27). It is the anchor for your soul (Hebrews 6:19). Hope will embolden you (2 Corinthians 3:12) and inspire endurance (1 Thessalonians 1:3).

Hope is Jesus Himself (1 Timothy 1:1).

> *We have this hope as an anchor for the soul,*
> *firm and secure (Hebrews 6:19).*

◦

What's Percolating in Me: My Response

_____

_____

_____

Spill the Beans: My Prayer

_____

_____

_____

Thanks a Latte! My Praise

_____

_____

_____

39

Instant Community

THE NINTENDO WII WAS THE ONE and only gift on my Connor's Christmas list that year.

He told me in July that he wanted one. He reminded me in September, and in November he flat out asked, "Mom, can I get a Wii for Christmas?"

Because it was a pricey item, I told him that if he wanted a Wii, it would be his only gift—to which he instantly agreed.

Confident that the gift was a done deal, he gleefully told everyone at school he was getting a Wii. The only problem was that nobody told me that everyone else in the United States of America was also intending to purchase a Wii that year.

So about the second week of December, I sauntered into my local superstore and naively asked the geeky guy behind the counter, "Can I please have a Wii?"

It was all he could do to contain his incredulity. I could detect his sincere attempt to compose himself as he replied with a quavery voice, "Ma'am, we don't have any. *Nobody* has any. You will need to show up when the truck arrives and stand in line just for a chance to get a Wii."

Since the trucks' arrival time differed from day to day and store to store, I decided to call first. Each day, I picked up my phone and called no less than seven stores (along with about seventy other shoppers) and asked about the Wii. It got to the point that operators wouldn't even connect me to the electronic or gaming department. They would simply say, "No truck yet. Come in around noon." I started to figure out that "come in around noon" was the party line for operators to state no matter what the question.

"Do you have any Wii's?"

"Come in around noon."

"Did anyone find a brown leather wallet? I think I left it there yesterday."

"Come in around noon."

"Are your honey-cured hams still on sale?"

"Come in around noon."

Finally, I got an idea. I knew there was a gaming store in the mall that was small and usually not very crowded. So I called them and got the same line but with a twist. "Our shipment arrives between ten and noon each day. We never know if any will be in the shipment, but you're welcome to come and wait."

So my mall stalking began on my forty-fourth birthday. I arrived, coffee in hand, to the gaming store where two clerks greeted me. They told me to wait behind the lady standing to their left. She was the first in line.

"I'm second," I said with a smile.

Surely today would be the day. Obtaining my youngest son's fondest Christmas wish would be the best birthday present I could receive. All the rest of my shopping was done, and this would release me from all remaining gift-buying anxiety.

I got to know the lady before me, getting the details about her kids, her Christmas plans, and her job. Together, we experienced a nervous tingle when the parcel service came lumbering into the store.

"They're here," she gasped.

I contained the urge to reach out and hold her hand for support. I found myself praying for a Wii to be on the cart among the 29 boxes.

The lady standing with me offered color commentary. "The clerk is rummaging through the boxes…he doesn't look good."

I moaned and kept hope alive. After all, I had been there almost two hours—just standing there, shifting my weight from foot to foot, sipping Starbucks, and visiting with my fellow mall stalker.

The clerk walked toward us.

"None," he said with finality. "We got none. Come back tomorrow. I'm sure we'll get some tomorrow."

We took our disappointed selves out of the store and dragged our feet out of the mall. "See ya tomorrow," she announced.

The next day, which was five days before Christmas, I awoke, put on my most comfortable shoes, and dressed in layers in case it was hot in the store. Loading my purse with chocolate and my iPod with an audio book, I breathed a prayer that the Wii would be there and stepped outside to face the elements.

Then I breathed another, asking God to forgive me for my materialism. If only Connor had wanted something else. A bike. An ant farm. An autographed football. Anything. But no, he wanted one thing, and one thing only. And I was determined to get it.

So I arrived at the game store at 9:30, assuming I was good and early. My secret hope was to beat the lady who had been first in line the day before. I liked her as a person, but as far as mall stalking goes, she was the competition, and it's every woman for herself.

When I arrived, however, I found three people already in line ahead of me. This was going to be a tough stalking experience. My friend from the day before greeted me, introducing me to the two men who were now before me. If there were just two boxes on that truck, we would each get a Wii, since they came two to a box. (Mall stalkers know these things.)

We chit-chatted among us, forming a tight little community right there in front of the cash registers. One man wanted a Wii for his nephew. Another guy was trying to get one to give away at his office Christmas party to be held that very afternoon. Of course, the lady from the day before wanted it for her nieces; she already had one for her boys. So I figured if situational ethics prevailed in the event of a Wii shortage, certainly the community would choose me—after all, I wanted a Wii for my little boy. And it was the only gift he wanted, the only gift he was getting.

But there were to be no situational ethics here, just survival of the fittest. The Christmas cheer in our little community in front of the registers was only a thin veneer, a polite glaze barely covering the fanatic, mall-stalking shoppers who weren't about to leave without a Wii.

Ten minutes passed. Twenty minutes. Time ticked away and so did my confidence. And then my color commentator friend announced, "He's here." By now, three more people were in line behind me, and we all became very tense and focused.

The parcel cart rolled up, loaded with boxes. "There's a lot of

Nintendo boxes," the line-leading lady confided. "Surely there are some Wii's in there." We all tried to act coy, but we weren't.

"He doesn't look as grim as yesterday," she added hopefully. "He's taking six boxes to the cash register."

"Does that mean there are 12 Wii's?" I asked in wonder.

"It must, it must, it must."

Just then, our nervous tension was shattered by the sales clerk's triumphant announcement: "If you're waiting for a Wii, come to the register."

We came, shuffling forward, patting each other on the back, congratulating one another. One by one, we laid down our money, tucked the coveted bag under our arms, and wished each other a happy Christmas as we departed the store.

I was thrilled I got the Wii, but I got something even better in the process. I got a glimpse of how little it takes to form community. It takes shared goals, proximity, and just a little commitment and interest in one another's lives and goals.

Now, isn't that what Christmas does? Isn't that what Christ does? Because He came into our lives, we can live in community. I had the strangest urge to hug the people in line with me after I got my Wii. It was mutual commitment, mutual success. Our joy was a shared joy, our victory shared in a way that only the truly desperate and stouthearted would understand.

That's community. And that's the heartbeat of New Testament Christianity.

And let us consider one another in order to stir up
love and good works, not forsaking the assembling
of ourselves together, as is the manner of some, but

exhorting one another, and so much the more as you see the Day approaching (Hebrews 10:24-25 NKJV).

What's Percolating in Me: My Response

_____

_____

_____

_____

Spill the Beans: My Prayer

_____

_____

_____

_____

Thanks a Latte! My Praise

_____

_____

_____

_____

40

A Tribute
to Thierry

EARLIER IN THIS BOOK, you read a chapter about my friend Thierry, who had been healed of brain cancer in 2000. I wrote of God's amazing resurrection power, and we marveled at His mercy in Thierry's life. And that was exactly what we should have done.

Well, a new year has come, and as of January 16, at 4:00 p.m., I now really understand what true healing looks like. My friend Thierry learned several months ago that the cancer had returned. Once again, he believed God for complete healing. After he faithfully fought, God mercifully healed. He traded Thierry's corruptible earth suit for the incorruptible garment of glory.

I am convinced that there is no one in heaven today celebrating louder than Thierry. I'll bet he busted through those pearly gates, whooping and hollering, knocking down patron saints as he ran into the arms of Jesus.

You see, on Thursday at 4:00 p.m., Thierry's faith did not cease; *his faith became sight.* Though we will all miss him deeply, we hold fast to his memory and to his God.

What remains, however, is an empty seat at the Kobes' family dinner table. What is left is an empty space in Diane's bed and in her heart. Nichole, age seven, will grow up much faster than we'd wish for her. Little Christian and baby Micah will know their daddy best only through stories and pictures.

What remains is very painful. The road they will travel will be difficult and dark at times. Our only solace is in the truth that the very road they walk will eventually lead them home. Even on the darkest days, the road will be illuminated by the peace and presence of Christ Himself.

You see, God understands the road Thierry traveled, and He understands the road Diane and the children will travel. He understands because He clothed Himself in humanity and walked our roads. He eventually walked the road called the Way of Suffering, which led Him to the cross. But on the other side of the cross was the resurrection.

The resurrection is what gives us hope. Hope chooses to keep the faith even on a deathbed. Hope strengthens the countenance of a widow.

Goodbye Thierry. I honor you my friend. Your time here was well spent. Thank you for teaching me a little more about faith and a lot about tenacity, and for reminding me that to be touched by loss and sadness is to be strengthened by hope.

Friend, you may have lost someone you love, and you understand so very well the emptiness that remains. May God's comfort and presence fill that space for you today. And if you know someone who has endured a great loss, be the comfort of God in her life today. As the Lord enables you, fill that aching empty place inside her...even if only for a few moments.

My soul, wait in silence for God only,
For my hope is from Him.
He only is my rock and my salvation,
My stronghold; I shall not be shaken.
On God my salvation and my glory rest;
The rock of my strength, my refuge is in God.
Trust in Him at all times, O people;
Pour out your heart before Him;
God is a refuge for us. Selah
(Psalm 62:5-8 NASB).

❧ What's Percolating in Me: My Response

_____

_____

❧ Spill the Beans: My Prayer

_____

_____

❧ Thanks a Latte! My Praise

_____

_____

41

Is God Punishing Me?

PHIL AND I WERE IN THE KITCHEN getting ready for another session of Connor's day camp when we heard our little camper heading into the kitchen. Our ears were alert because his arrivals were recently accompanied by a stuffy nose, itchy eyes, and coughs galore. On this particular morning, he also awoke with an inquisitive mind.

"Mom, am I still sick because God is punishing me?"

I couldn't believe my ears. I could just see Phil's thought bubble forming above his head as he casually stood by the table: *I am so glad he started the question with "Mom" and not "Dad"!*

Where in the world did he get such a notion? my thought bubble read.

"No, honey," I reassured. "Just because you are sick doesn't mean God is punishing you."

"Well then, why do we get sick anyway?" Connor persisted.

As I moved his cereal bowl to the kitchen table, I was struck with the profound nature of the question and the simple answer it demanded.

"Connor," I began "it's all because of the Garden of Eden. Do you remember what happened there?"

"Oh yeah—Eve ate the apple and they found out they were naked."

The chuckles from his dad and me confirmed that he rightly summed it up. But even so, I continued to fumble through the mystery of how God intended that our lives would be just like that beautiful garden, but when Adam and Eve chose to disobey God, sin entered our world. Because of sin, everything that was supposed to be perfect became imperfect. Everything that was whole became broken. Everything that was eternal and beautiful started to decay and fade.

"Does that make sense, Connor?" I asked.

"Uh-huh." He grabbed his backpack and joined his dad at the door. Phil simply breathed a quiet "I can't believe he asked that question" as he kissed me goodbye.

Both Phil and I were baffled as well as amused by his question. I was also relieved that Connor, at least for now, was satisfied with the answer I gave. But here's the deal. Someday, he will consider the question with a far more mature mind. He will examine the innate wrongness he feels about the suffering in the world. He will look at his mom's blindness through eyes that seek to reconcile God's goodness with the faith of his family. He will someday have to sift through our feeble human myths and explanations. He will look back to the kitchen table when he was only six years old and find a degree of satisfaction in his simple yet profound theology: "Oh yeah—Eve ate the apple and they found out they were naked."

It is true that the choice made in the garden allowed sin and its consequent suffering to become part and parcel of our fallen world. Sin opened the door for the unwelcome visitors of sickness, violence, and myriad other awful human maladies that assault us. But the Creator of the garden is the re-Creator of our lives. What we lost in the garden, God bought back on the cross. Our Redeemer redeems every part of our lives.

Don't let the enemy rope you into believing the myth that your sickness is always God's punishment. Let God redeem that lie, for in doing so, He redeems the suffering.

My friend, God loves you. Let your sickness or hardship—whether you make sense of it or not—become a bridge that draws you to God rather than a wall that separates you from Him.

*For as in Adam all die, so in Christ all will
be made alive (1 Corinthians 15:22).*

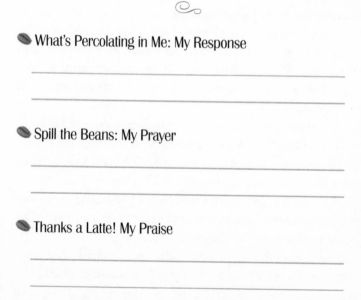

What's Percolating in Me: My Response

_____

_____

Spill the Beans: My Prayer

_____

_____

Thanks a Latte! My Praise

_____

_____

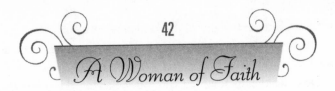

42

A Woman of Faith

ALPHA GOOMBI WANTED TO BE the first Native American actress to win an Academy Award. I wasn't surprised at all to learn this about her. As I experienced her presentation of an incredibly dramatic and moving production in her full Native American regalia, I was blown away by her intensity and talent.

"Alphie" and I have shared the platform at women's conferences and shared time together in my home as she and her husband, Ron, visited our church for missions conferences.

Alphie received Christ when she was 27 years old. She grew up in a family that endured many of the same difficulties many other Native American families have endured—sexual abuse, poverty, alcohol, and prejudice.

"I had a very painful life before my conversion, and I am able to share truthfully with people who are lost and hurting," Alphie said during one of our first conversations. "I want to serve God because of what He's done in my life."

And that's exactly what she does in Omaha, Nebraska, as a missionary to the Native American community along with her husband, Ron, and their boys.

I remember the night, however, when I received a troubling phone call from a friend. "Did you hear about Alphie?" she asked.

"No, what happened?"

My friend had few details. She knew just enough to make my heart begin to break. I immediately called Alphie to find out what happened. "Oh, Alphie...I just heard the worst news. Please tell me it's not true."

"It's true," she said and then told me the awful story. Her father, Billy Evan Horse, was in a truck, driving just a few cars in front of the minivan that carried Alphie's mother, her sister, Helen, and her 17-year-old cousin, Rose.

The Oklahoma rains had been falling, and the flood waters had risen dangerously high. The surging waters had pushed the truck into a guardrail, where it got stuck. Alphie's father tried to warn the approaching minivan to stop, but the women in the van didn't see his frantic signal and continued to drive, passing her frightened father.

The van was caught up in the current and washed into a pond, where it submerged. The three women apparently tried to get out but couldn't. When they realized they were trapped, they embraced in the backseat of the van, where they died together.

Alphie told me the story on her cell phone as she and Ron were on their way to the funeral. The sadness I felt for Alphie and her father was overwhelming. The respect I have for Alphie as a faithful woman of God is also overwhelming. Alphie has endured sorrows and disadvantages in life that many would have allowed to discourage them. Many have turned their back on their faith for far lesser tragedy than Alphie has been through.

My friend Alpha Goombi may not be the first Native American actress to win an Academy Award, but she will most certainly receive a reward that poverty can't penetrate, storms can't wash away, and tragedy can't touch. Our faithful God keeps His eyes on His faithful children, and Alpha is one of them.

You be faithful too. Be encouraged today, my friend. Pray for those who are in pain and be faithful to love God and trust Him even with the disappointments.

> *Blessed is the man who perseveres under trial,*
> *because when he has stood the test, he will receive*
> *the crown of life that God has promised to those*
> *who love him (James 1:12).*

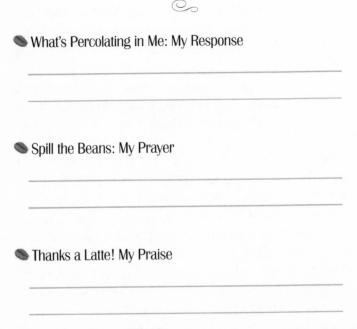

What's Percolating in Me: My Response

_____

_____

Spill the Beans: My Prayer

_____

_____

Thanks a Latte! My Praise

_____

_____

43

The Weight of Peace

THERE'S JUST SOMETHING ABOUT GETTING UP EARLY and being the only one awake in my house. I love it. It's the perfect kind of quiet—not so silent that I feel totally isolated, just a simple, uncluttered, contented sort of peace. The hum of the refrigerator pads the quiet with an assurance of a steadiness, an unchanging reality that always exists, even when all seems tumultuous.

I am amazed that peace can coexist with all the other feelings in my heart and chaos in my home.

I remember one truly stressful season—and one peculiarly quiet morning in the midst of it—when Phil had a research paper looming. While he was supposed to be writing it, we were launching a website, updating my newsletter, and finalizing the purchase of our new house.

Oh, and moving too, by the way. Talk about stressful.

Clay was getting over the stomach flu as he slept in the next bedroom, Connor had day camp that following week, and I was the one packing the house and hiring all the movers, cleaners, painters, and carpet layers.

As I sat alone in the silence of the early morning, I was well aware of the weight of this particular slice of our family's life together. But at the same time, I was also well aware of God's peace that stays with me and sustains me through each and every season.

When things are truly upside-down in our world, by all rights, by all logic, we shouldn't be peaceful. But against all odds, we can be. How thankful I am.

I don't understand such peace. I don't *have* to understand such peace. And neither do you.

The Bible speaks of "the peace of God, which surpasses all understanding" (Philippians 4:7 NKJV). The passage goes on to say that His peace will keep or guard our minds as we trust in Him.

It's not so much about pursuing peace; it's more about pursuing trust and faith, and finding peace as the result. I know your burden may feel heavy today. You may feel the weight of stress bearing down on your life, my friend. But the peace of God is a perfect counterweight that can lift the heaviest of hearts. Trust Him today to give you the peace that passes your understanding and transcends your chaos.

May the God of hope fill you with joy and peace in your faith, that by the power of the Holy Spirit, your whole life and outlook may be radiant with hope (Romans 15:13 PHILLIPS).

What's Percolating in Me: My Response

_____

_____

_____

_____

Spill the Beans: My Prayer

_____

_____

_____

_____

Thanks a Latte! My Praise

_____

_____

_____

_____

44

An Unreserved Yes

JESUS HAD BEEN BUSY PREACHING AND HEALING. Word of His ministry and mighty works had spread throughout the region, and two blind men caught wind of what the Nazarene was doing.

They pursued Him.

Tracking Him through the city and pushing their way through crowds, they boldly entered the house where the Teacher had gone to rest.

Before you pass this off as Sunday school 101, think about it. These guys were *blind*. As someone who is pretty accustomed to the trappings of blindness, let me shed some light on this picture. The blind leading the blind may be a descriptive colloquialism, but in real life it's practically impossible.

But that's what was happening here. With no one to guide them, these determined friends negotiated crowds and unfamiliar parts of the city. They must have constantly struggled to stay oriented because of the distracting noises of the excitable crowd. They wanted to meet Jesus so much that they were willing to look foolish, risk their pride, ask for help, and not give up. Couldn't we all use a dose of that kind of spiritual perseverance?

When they finally reached Jesus inside a home, they showed great respect by calling Him "Son of David," demonstrating their faith by their sheer tenacity.

Yet isn't it interesting how Jesus responded to them? He looked at them and said, "Do you believe I am able to do this?"

To me that seems like a no-brainer! Of course they believed! They followed after Him against all odds. They fought through darkness, dead ends, and untold dangers to present themselves in His presence. You don't do that unless you believe, right?

Sometimes I'm afraid I push my belief in Christ's ability to answer prayer to the very edge. I don't ask Him to do anything outside my comfort zone. Why? Because...well, I guess I want to protect Him.

Silly isn't it? Maybe I think to myself, *What if He doesn't heal, even though He is able? Will He appear unkind? Will I look foolish for asking?*

And therein lies the real crisis of belief. The problem is not with Him. The only problem is with my perception of Him. When Jesus confronted the two blind men concerning their level of belief, they affirmed it without hesitation. As a result, they both left their canes at the door and walked out into the bright sunlight of a new season of life. They were healed.

We all experience a similar crisis of belief. Sometimes we are unwilling to ask God for things because we are uncertain of how He will answer. Yet the answer we should be most concerned about is our own.

When we examine our prayer list, we might hear a still small voice echo through the chambers of our minds, *Do you believe I am able?* Our answer should be *yes!* Just like the blind men, we express our belief through our actions. So whatever you need from God today, ask Him for it. Lay your hope and desire on the altar of belief, for that is a sacrifice that pleases God. Be more concerned with your answer to Him than His answer to you. For when we offer an unreserved yes to God, we receive the blessing He has reserved for us.

And all things you ask in prayer, believing,
you will receive (Matthew 21:22 NASB).

What's Percolating in Me: My Response

_____
_____
_____

Spill the Beans: My Prayer

_____
_____
_____

Thanks a Latte! My Praise

_____
_____
_____

45

I Love People

CONNOR SAT DOWN WITH A BRAND-NEW collector's notebook. It had hundreds of pages, each with dozens of slots for his thousands of cards. I just knew this project would occupy his busy nine-year-old body and brain for hours.

It was a holiday weekend, and Connor needed something to keep him busy. He had just finished marveling about his new notebook, laying out all the pages on the bar to begin stuffing them, when his big brother walked in the door.

Clayton called out, "Mom, Mason and Wesley are here."

That's all it took. Connor sprung from his barstool, left the new notebook and slick pages behind, and gleefully announced, "I *love* people!"

He bolted toward the door, grabbing his jacket on the way, and continued, "That means I'm an extrovert, right, Mom? I love being an extrovert."

Solitude pulls the life out of Connor. But bring one human into his sphere, *any* human, and his former wither begins to bud. People are like sparks who ignite his inner fire. They warm him and energize him.

I am an introvert who loves to watch my extroverted son, and I enjoy him enjoying people. As an introvert, I get my energy from some well-timed, quality solitude.

How about you? Are you an introvert or extrovert? God made each of us uniquely *us*. If you are an extrovert, love being one! If you need a little more quiet and introspection, celebrate that. It's how God chose to design you. Tune in to what energizes you, and make sure you get plenty of it. Pay attention to what makes you tick. Recognize your strengths, weaknesses, and those particular personality nuances that help you to live well the life God has granted you.

I praise you because I am fearfully and
wonderfully made;
your works are wonderful,
I know that full well (Psalm 139:14).

What's Percolating in Me: My Response

_____

_____

Spill the Beans: My Prayer

_____

_____

Thanks a Latte! My Praise

_____

_____

46

Savoring
the Beauty

DURING MY JUNIOR YEAR OF COLLEGE, I was transported to a place of wonder.

It happened in an unlikely setting—an old, musty classroom in Borbe Hall. In my British literature class, Dr. Blakemore settled in a chair beside the podium, pulled out a worn, dog-eared book of poetry, and began to read "Ode on a Grecian Urn."

The John Keats poem he read with such loving reverence awakened an appreciation and a need for beauty within me that had lain dormant for years. I couldn't really explain why his tone, pausing, sighs, and almost whisper of some of those almost 200-year-old lines spun such webs of wonder around me. It was a turning point in my life, though I really can't explain why. All I know is I have never forgotten it.

Well, actually, the memory had fallen to an obscure place in my mind until recently as I read C.S. Lewis' autobiography, *Surprised by Joy*. Lewis writes of his school days and harkens back to one of his most poignant recollections. He speaks warmly of his "honey-tongued" teacher, whom the students called Smugie. He was crowned with gray hair and wore spectacles, and every word on his lips turned to music…something midway between speech and song.

Lewis credited his old schoolmaster with introducing him to the enchantment of poetry—how it should be "savored and mouthed in solitude." Smugie once told his students concerning a particular line from Milton, "That line made me happy for a week."

It got me to thinking—have I read or experienced something so beautiful lately that it "made me happy for a week"? What I heard in that classroom more than 20 years ago made me happy—truly happy—with that particular kind of happiness that is less a feeling and more a recognition of the transcendent. Decades later, my professor's reading of Keats's line, "Beauty is truth, truth beauty" still haunts me. It has brought me happiness for decades.

Beauty is intended to bring happiness. But it's up to us to look, listen, observe, feel, and participate with its presentation. Lewis says, "Beauty is not democratic; she reveals herself more to the few than to the many."

I want to be part of that privileged minority, don't you?

Oh, to savor the revelation of beauty…to feel deep eternal happiness in its wake.

> *One thing I ask of the LORD,*
> *   this is what I seek:*
> *that I may dwell in the house of the LORD*
> *   all the days of my life,*
> *to gaze upon the beauty of the LORD*
> *and to seek him in his temple (Psalm 27:4).*

What's Percolating in Me: My Response

_____

_____

_____

_____

Spill the Beans: My Prayer

_____

_____

_____

_____

Thanks a Latte! My Praise

_____

_____

_____

_____

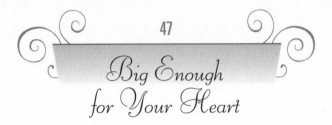

47

Big Enough
for Your Heart

I RECEIVED AN E-MAIL WITH A QUESTION that set me back a bit.

"How big is heaven?"

I went to Scripture to find the answer, and what I discovered was interesting—but not nearly as interesting as what I discovered in my own heart.

The Bible speaks of a new heaven and a new earth in Revelation 21:1, and who could begin to imagine the vastness of these realms? God is infinite, so perhaps His dwelling will be infinite as well. That's really what I would expect, wouldn't you?

In the very next verse, however, the apostle John speaks of "the Holy City, the new Jerusalem, coming down out of heaven from God."

And that city, at least, is measurable. Revelation 21–22 state that the size of the holy city is about 1400 miles long, wide, and high. According to experts, this amount of space is equivalent to almost two thirds of the land mass of the United States. In addition to that, the wall of the heavenly city described in Revelation is 1400 miles high. That's an incredibly towering wall when you consider that most commercial airliners fly at an altitude of only about six miles above the earth.

But do the numbers and measurements of Revelation work the same way our numbers and measurements do today? Are these literal measurements or figurative language representing a larger truth? I'm no mathematician, and no theologian either, for that matter.

I really don't know the exact size of the heavenly city, let alone heaven itself. And I don't have to know. Neither do you.

Oh yes, there's been all kinds of speculation through the centuries about the specifics and dimensions of the realm to come. How big is heaven? I have my own answer that suits me just fine.

Heaven is bigger than my sin, bigger than my imagination, bigger than my failure, bigger than my hopes, bigger than my loss, bigger than I deserve. Heaven is as huge as God's heart and as vast as His forgiveness. Heaven is as gigantic as His grace and as immense as His benevolence. Heaven is as enormous as His holiness, as cosmic as His care for us, and as measureless as His mercy.

The writer of the eighth-century Irish poem "Be Thou My Vision" knew the size of heaven because he knew the King of heaven:

> High King of heaven, my victory won
> May I reach heaven's joys, O bright heaven's Sun.
> Heart of my own heart, whatever befall,
> Still be my Vision, O Ruler of all.

Everything I discovered in Scripture about heaven confirms what my heart has discovered as I too have walked with the King of heaven.

Heaven is big...big enough to fit in your heart.

But as it is written:
"Eye has not seen, nor ear heard,
nor have entered into the heart of man
the things which God has prepared for
those who love Him" (1 Corinthians 2:9 NKJV).

❧

What's Percolating in Me: My Response

_____

_____

_____

Spill the Beans: My Prayer

_____

_____

_____

Thanks a Latte! My Praise

_____

_____

_____

48

Broken Once,
Forever One

MY FAVORITE AUTHOR, C.S. LEWIS, wrote the following words about a book he came across as a young man: "It must be more than thirty years ago that I bought *Phantastes*...A few hours later I knew I had crossed a great frontier. What it actually did to me was to convert, even to baptize my imagination."

The book was by George McDonald—and that was all I needed to hear. I had to find and read a book by one of my favorite author's favorite authors! And when I found such a book, I knew I had found a storehouse of treasure.

I found my first MacDonald book online and began listening to the digital voice of my computer read it to me. In spite of the monotone rendition, my imagination was transported to a place I'd never been before, and since being there, I am forever changed.

The book was *The Princess and the Goblin* (1872)—supposedly a child's fairy tale, but it captivated this woman's sense of wonder.

The story includes an interesting exchange between Grandmother and Princess Irene that has stayed with me.

> "But in the meantime you must be content, I say,
> to be misunderstood for a while. We are all very
> anxious to be understood, and it is very hard not to
> be. But there is one thing much more necessary."
>
> "What is that, Grandmother?"
>
> "To understand other people."
>
> "Yes, Grandmother. I must be fair—for if I'm not
> fair to other people, I'm not worth being under-
> stood myself."

The innocent insight of seeking understanding rather than simply being understood is a concept found in MacDonald's tale but lost in our "it's all about me" generation. Each of us longs to be understood. Yet to be misunderstood—seeking understanding instead—allows us to identify with our Savior in a unique and unparalleled way.

It seems to me that if the body of Christ applied more of Grandmother's admonishment to Irene, we would be characterized by a wonderful unity rather than splinters and divisions.

The body of Christ was broken on the cross for us once on a dark day at Golgotha. To choose disunity is to break His body—the church—again. He was broken so we would be one whole body.

For that reason, let us not demand understanding; rather let us seek to understand. Let each of us extend the mercy we hope to receive to others with whom we might disagree.

To achieve unity in the body of Christ, we knit ourselves together. Unity does not mean we become uniform and settle for unanimity. The beauty of His Body is revealed in the way our diversity is woven into one tapestry of truth.

Our Savior was broken so we could be one. Don't allow His precious body to be broken again. Being understood isn't really the treasure you long for. The real treasure comes with sweet unity between your brothers and sisters in Christ.

> *Holy Father, keep them in Your name, the name*
> *which You have given Me, that they may be one*
> *even as We are (John 17:11 NASB).*

❧ What's Percolating in Me: My Response

_____

_____

_____

❧ Spill the Beans: My Prayer

_____

_____

_____

❧ Thanks a Latte! My Praise

_____

_____

_____

49

Building on
the Foundation

SUMMER IS HOME IMPROVEMENT TIME at the Rothschild homestead. One year, when Phil and I began to assess all the projects that needed to be done around our home, it prompted us to go look at new houses! We figured that by the time we invested all of that time and money updating our floors, walls, and fixtures, we might as well buy a new house.

So we joined the many curious onlookers who marched through Springfield's Parade of Homes. We saw everything from modest to magnificent, and as we toured, we took careful note of the differences between builders. We could visibly recognize where each builder invested his capital and what was most important to him.

You know how we could tell, don't you? It was clear by the quality of the building materials they used. Some laid granite countertops in the kitchen, some laid Formica. In some homes, we trod upon the most lovely parquet wood floors, in others, it was linoleum. I am quite sure though, that the part of each home that we could not see, the foundation, was much the same. For me as a novice house hunter, the quality of the building materials I could see was a reflection of the quality of the foundation I could not see.

The same is true, my friend, with you and me. The quality of the building materials we use in our lives reflects the foundation we build our lives on. Paul put it best in his letter to the Corinthians:

> For no one can lay any foundation other than the one already laid, which is Jesus Christ. If any man builds on this foundation using gold, silver, costly stones, wood, hay or straw, his work will be shown for what it is, because the Day will bring it to light. It will be revealed with fire, and the fire will test the quality of each man's work. If what he has built survives, he will receive his reward (1 Corinthians 3:11-14).

The building supplies Paul mentions have something in common. They each have an assigned value. Gold, silver, and precious stones cost a great deal. They require sacrifice in order to obtain them, and they don't seem to lose their value. Wood, hay, and straw, on the other hand, are easy to obtain, with little or no value. Each is easily accessible, requiring little or no effort or sacrifice.

So when I survey the building materials in these verses, I am prompted to survey the building materials in my life. I wonder... what do I build with? Does it cost me anything? Is it enduring? Am I a cheap builder? Do I offer to God that which costs me nothing? Do you?

I don't want to be a stick gatherer. I really don't want to invest my life in collecting cheap pieces of straw and stubble to build on the foundation of Christ's finished work in my life. If Jesus is my foundation of solid gold, I don't want to build my walls with Legos.

I must build on the foundation of my life with the costly stones of sacrifice, the purest gold of godliness, and the sterling silver quality of servanthood.

Paul tells us that the fire of judgment will eventually reveal the quality of the building materials we chose. But it seems to me that the refining fire of trials we experience here and now can reveal a lot about our buildings also. The works of wood, the habits of hay, and the service of straw never endure when the fire is hot. They are the transient and feeble building materials of graceless giving, merciless ministering, and selfish serving.

When the heat is on, they won't stand. You and I must be builders of quality construction because only what is built out of precious and costly materials will last. And the quality of the materials we use is a reflection of the foundation of our lives.

The heavenly reward of which Paul writes can be experienced—in some measure—on this side of heaven. I believe we find it in the ability to enjoy the lasting nature of that which we sacrificed—realizing that the cost is worth it and the Foundation deserves it.

So, my friend, build well.

When the whirlwind passes, the wicked is no more,
But the righteous has an everlasting foundation
(Proverbs 10:25 NASB).

❧ What's Percolating in Me: My Response

❧ Spill the Beans: My Prayer

❧ Thanks a Latte! My Praise

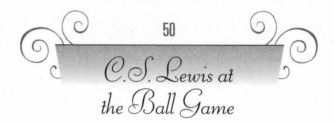

50

C.S. Lewis at the Ball Game

LAST WEEKEND I JOINED MY HUSBAND and two sons at a Kansas City Royals game. The weather was perfect, the fans were excited, and the food was phenomenal. The whole atmosphere was delightful and electric.

I had a marvelous time, but not because of the reasons I've mentioned. For me, it was marvelous because of the fourth man who joined us at the game. His name was C.S. Lewis.

You see, my family was graciously given tickets to the afternoon game against the Minnesota Twins, and my guys were thrilled. I, on the other hand, was thrilled only for them. I don't enjoy baseball. For whatever reason, I just can't get into sitting in a stiff stadium seat for four hours while the sun beats mercilessly down on my head. To me, a baseball game is simply an unsolicited opportunity to obtain an unwanted farmer's tan and quickly fade the chestnut brown from my color-treated hair.

So before my trip, I lamented my plight to my assistant. Ever helpful, she came back with a suggestion. "Why don't you get a book on tape?" she said. "You can hide the Walkman and slip an earbud beneath your hair. No one will be the wiser."

Oh, brilliant idea!

So off to the Christian bookstore we went, and after moments of shopping, I became the proud owner of *Mere Christianity* by C.S. Lewis. I had read excerpts from this classic over the years, but I had never listened to the entire book. I was pumped.

So when game time arrived, I couldn't wait. I impatiently settled in my seat and kept checking my watch. I enjoyed the singing of our anthem and marveled at the hush that fell on the stadium as the fans solemnly stood with hands over their hearts. But then, with the last note, the crowd erupted in applause, the game began, and I pressed play.

For the next four hours—while the boys in white and blue swung at inside curves, stole bases, and dove for fly balls—I listened, pondered, and silently praised my God who led Lewis to write such a rich work.

So growing out of that delightful experience, here's my suggestion to you: When the task ahead of you is less than thrilling, don't go it alone. Bring someone with you! Bring someone you can listen to, someone who tells you things worth pondering, and someone who prompts you to praise.

In case you're thinking I'm only referring to C.S. Lewis, I want you to know this someone isn't purchased from a bookstore and confined to a Walkman. No, this someone is the Holy Spirit. He's freely given to you and is available to accompany you everywhere you go. Press Play today, tune in to His presence, and listen. He will make the atmosphere of your life truly delightful and electric.

Remember the words of Jesus:

But when the Father sends the Advocate as my representative—that is, the Holy Spirit—he will teach you everything and will remind you of everything I myself have told you (John 14:26 NLT).

⚬

🫘 What's Percolating in Me: My Response

_____

_____

_____

🫘 Spill the Beans: My Prayer

_____

_____

_____

🫘 Thanks a Latte! My Praise

_____

_____

_____

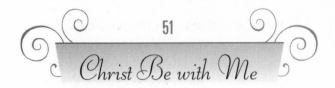

51

Christ Be with Me

MORE THAN 1500 YEARS AGO, a young man named Maewyn
Succat lived in Wales with his Anglo-Roman family. When he
was only 16 years old, he was captured by an Irish pagan warlord
known as Niall of the Nine Hostages.

Maewyn was carried away against his will to Ireland, separated from his family, and forced into slavery for six long years.
What must those years have been like? Lonely? Confusing? Did
that time of harsh slavery make him question the God in whom
he had believed? Did the internment lead him to detest the country in which he found himself?

By the time he was about 23, he was able to escape. Evidently
his time in Ireland didn't pull him from his God but rather drew
him to God, because he became a priest and changed his name
to Patricius, or Patrick, which comes from the Latin word meaning "father-figure" or "patrician, patron." Rather than ignoring
the horrors of slavery or forgetting his wretched experiences in
Ireland, he willingly went back to the country where he had
been enslaved.

He spent his later years preaching Christianity to the Irish
and telling them about the Savior who had been with him during
his six years of slavery.

He introduced the Irish to the triune God using the shamrock.

He used this three-leafed clover to help put the concept of the Trinity in plain words—how God could be three persons—and yet one.

This man, whom we now know as St. Patrick, is believed to have died in 493, and his remains are assumed to be buried in a grave at Down Cathedral in Downpatrick.

His legacy, however, goes far beyond clovers, symbols, and Irish nationalism. Patrick left footprints of faith in which we should follow. He understood that Christ was with him regardless of where he was. He saw his risen Lord in everything and everyone around him. He allowed his slavery to be redeemed for the good and salvation of the Irish people, and today we are still inspired by his faithful expression of trust in God.

Some poignant words he wrote still remain. May they be a blessing to you today.

> I bind unto myself today
> The strong name of the Trinity,
> By invocation of the same,
> The Three in One, and One in Three.
>
> I bind this day to me for ever,
> By power of faith, Christ's incarnation,
> His baptism in the Jordan river,
> His death on cross for my salvation,
> His bursting from the spiced tomb,
> His riding up the heavenly way,
> His coming at the day of doom:
> I bind unto myself today.
>
> I bind unto myself today

The virtues of the star-lit heaven,
The glorious sun's life-giving ray,
The whiteness of the moon at even,
The flashing of the lightning free,
The whirling wind's tempestuous shocks,
The stable earth, the deep salt sea,
Around the old eternal rocks.

I bind unto myself today
The power of God to hold and lead,
His eye to watch, his might to stay,
His ear to hearken to my need,
The wisdom of my God to teach,
His hand to guide, his shield to ward,
The word of God to give me speech,
His heavenly host to be my guard.

Christ be with me, Christ within me,
Christ behind me, Christ before me,
Christ beside me, Christ to win me,
Christ to comfort and restore me,
Christ beneath me, Christ above me,
Christ in quiet, Christ in danger,
Christ in hearts of all that love me,
Christ in mouth of friend and stranger.

I bind unto myself today
The strong name of the Trinity,
By invocation of the same,
The Three in One, and One in Three
Of whom all nature hath creation,

Eternal Father, Spirit, Word,
Praise to the Lord of my salvation:
Salvation is of Christ the Lord.

*Father, I want those you have given me to be with
me where I am, and to see my glory, the glory you
have given me because you loved me before the
creation of the world (John 17:24).*

🫘 What's Percolating in Me: My Response

_____

_____

🫘 Spill the Beans: My Prayer

_____

_____

🫘 Thanks a Latte! My Praise

_____

_____

52

Ctrl-Z

I HAVE NOW ENTERED THE WORLD of computer mania, and I am quickly becoming a computer maniac. Mere months ago (could it really be?) I had never touched a computer. In fact, I didn't even know how to type. But last fall I was given a laptop and software that talks, and I was introduced to a nice man named Bill who has patiently trained me to use it all.

(No, not Bill Gates.)

Of all the many and varied things I have learned in computer land, the most valuable is the key command Ctrl-Z. You see, my early days on the keyboard were full of mistakes.

Some mistakes were minor and easily fixed by a touch of the Backspace key. But other blunders weren't quite as inconsequential.

Before Bill taught me the Ctrl-Z command, I had painstakingly typed in all the outlines to the messages I was to present for the LifeWay film project of my book *Fingerprints of God*.

This process took me hours upon hours. I was thrilled with my success. Now my computer could read me every word of all seven messages. I could review, ponder, and memorize each word I heard as I scrolled down using my well-worn arrow keys. I had never enjoyed such freedom and independence, and I was so excited.

Well, evidently my excitement got the best of me.

To this day I don't know exactly what I did, or how I did it, but somehow my computer started reading me the entire content of all the messages. In my ignorance, I listened in amusement until I got tired of hearing it all. It wouldn't stop! Somewhere in the middle of the third message, I started hitting random keys in an attempt to quiet my software.

It worked. The computer became silent. Deathly silent.

I pressed my arrow keys to hear where it had left the cursor. I expected to hear it pick up somewhere within the third message. But all it said was "blank, blank."

I scrolled up and down with my arrow keys. All I heard was "blank, blank." That's when panic gripped me. What had I done? I didn't know much, but I knew this couldn't be good! When my resident computer expert arrived home from high school, I quickly explained my quandary.

He moaned. "Oh Mom, you selected all and you *deleted* all."

"Can you fix it?" I asked with little hope.

"Not now, Mom. The damage is done." It was then he asked if I had learned about Ctrl-Z yet.

You can guess the very next question I asked Bill. "What is Ctrl-Z anyway?" With solemnity in his voice, Bill expressed regret that we had not discussed it earlier.

Why does Ctrl-Z matter so much anyway? It means "undo."

Now *that's* a key command I wish I could use in my everyday life. Wouldn't it be great if God had equipped us each with an undo button?

When I'm impatient with my boys…Ctrl-Z.

When I snap at my husband…Ctrl-Z.

When I forget a birthday or neglect a friend, when I gossip or overeat, when I am selfish or insulting…Ctrl-Z.

It sounds heavenly…I think. But what would it really mean if I had an undo button securely fastened to my life? Would I become more careless with my tongue or my actions? Very possibly! In fact, if I had such a Ctrl-Z I might not rely on the *real* control, the Holy Spirit, who indwells my life.

God doesn't give us an undo button, but He does give us His Spirit. His Spirit within us bears the fruit of self-control. If I live by the Spirit, I will not fulfill the desires of the flesh. If I allow Him to bear His sweet fruit of self-control in my life, I won't need an undo button.

Unfortunately, we can't undo the regrettable things we have done in life. What's done, as they say, is done. What's said, unfortunately, is said. But if we rely on the Spirit's control, we will have *fewer* things we wish we could undo! And with God's Spirit guiding me, I have the opportunity for *re*-dos. I can bring thoughtful words instead of harmful ones. I can offer kindness instead of indifference. I can infuse my minutes and hours with faith and confidence rather than negativity or fear.

And besides all that, I do think that there is ultimately a sovereign Ctrl-Z.

God's mercy is new every morning! One day we will stand before Him in heaven and the things of earth will be no more. All of our scars, regrets, sighs, and might-have-beens will fade in the light of His mercy and acceptance. God will once and for all Ctrl-Z all the hurts, sorrows, and disappointments of our life on earth. The prophet Isaiah speaks of a coming day when "the former things will not be remembered, nor will they come to mind" (Isaiah 65:17).

I guess, when I really consider it, I'm glad that I don't have a Ctrl-Z button fastened to my life. My mistakes make me grateful for His mercy. My blunders make me aware of His blessings, and my inability to undo makes me desperate for His sweet Holy Spirit's control in my life.

> *But what happens when we live God's way? He brings gifts into our lives, much the same way that fruit appears in an orchard—things like affection for others, exuberance about life, serenity. We develop a willingness to stick with things, a sense of compassion in the heart, and a conviction that a basic holiness permeates things and people. We find ourselves involved in loyal commitments, not needing to force our way in life, able to marshal and direct our energies wisely (Galatians 5:22-23 MSG).*

What's Percolating in Me: My Response

_____

_____

_____

_____

Spill the Beans: My Prayer

_____

_____

_____

_____

Thanks a Latte! My Praise

_____

_____

_____

_____

53

Questions but No Doubt

I DON'T RECALL ever doubting God.

Have you? Do you?

Looking back, tracing the long, winding path I've traveled since the onset of blindness, I've stumbled into plenty of potholes along the way. But I can't think of a time when I've fallen into *that* particular pothole. I don't condemn anyone who has wrestled with doubt, but for me, it hasn't been a struggle. Honestly, I can't remember a time when I doubted God's love, His character, or His goodness.

But I have asked Him plenty of hard questions! To me, there's a difference.

In my mind, to doubt is to cast suspicion or distrust on His character—or to even flirt with thoughts of His existence. To question, on the other hand, means I'm seeking to understand Him, His purpose, and my participation in a circumstance that He has allowed.

My lack of doubt is because of an abundance of grace and the gift of faith, not because of any extraordinary spiritual valor on my part. Just grace. My willingness to ask questions of God without demanding answers or questioning His good character is a result of the same—grace.

In a recent interview with *Decision* magazine, I put it like this:

> One of the hardest concepts to grasp is the fact that God actually uses painful circumstances in our lives for good.
>
> My hero, Joni Eareckson Tada, who has been in a wheelchair since she was a teenager, makes this point well when she says that God allows what He hates in order to accomplish what He loves. I know that God's heart is broken when He sees our hearts break.
>
> I believe that just as Jesus wept at Lazarus's tomb, Jesus weeps when He sees us cry tears of loss. I'm convinced that God is well acquainted with the sorrow and struggles that I experience. Yet at the same time, He loves me enough—and this is why I'm so loyal to Him—to let me encounter sorrow, taste bitter emotions, and feel loss, and to trust me to be a good steward of that sorrow. He loves me enough to let me experience that pain so that He can accomplish something He loves—which includes creating in me a deeper character and a more eternal perspective.
>
> I am convinced that God's grace has sustained me. If healing were sufficient, God would have provided it. If deliverance were sufficient, God would have delivered me. But He's allowed me to live with blindness

and yet live equally with the sufficiency of His grace, and that grace shows up in different ways on different days. But in whatever way it shows up, it has always been truly sufficient. It may never be well with our circumstances, but through God's grace, it can always be well with our souls.

My friend, invite God's grace to turn your doubts into dependence today, and may it always be well with your soul.

> *But because God was so gracious, so very generous, here I am. And I'm not about to let his grace go to waste (1 Corinthians 15:10 MSG).*

❧

● What's Percolating in Me: My Response

_____

_____

● Spill the Beans: My Prayer

_____

_____

● Thanks a Latte! My Praise

_____

_____

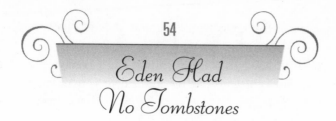

54

Eden Had No Tombstones

IT SEEMS THAT AGING IS OUR FRIEND when we first become aware of our existence on this planet. It holds our hands and ushers us through the seasons of infancy, toddlerhood, and childhood, delivering us into adulthood fully equipped. Age provides for us. It grants us opportunities, experience, change, and maturity.

As the calendar turns, however (and turns and turns and turns), aging loses most of its amusement. When we turn 30, for instance, we begin to anticipate the years with a little more circumspection. Aging has given us that glance into our future. As we move into our forties and through our fifties, aging still might be considered an ally, granting us the wisdom of experience and the benefit of 20/20 hindsight! It encourages us to feel more comfortable in our own skin, even if it's sagging to depths we've not plumbed before.

Aging gives us a reason to laugh at ourselves, a reason to appreciate our ownership of what is truly good in our lives, and it gives us the confidence to weed out that which had previously choked us.

So step forward and identify yourself, Aging! Are you friend or foe? Or are you friend *turned into* foe? Are you an ally, or are you like a double agent, handing us over to frailty and infirmity, our enemies?

After all, aging places us in a sandwich generation, where we find ourselves trying to care for both elderly parents and young children. Then it moves us on to empty nests, walkers, wheelchairs, and eventually, nursing homes.

It abandons us to the confines of a body that won't serve us well, sometimes allowing our brain to recognize our own limitations.

Aging used to be the thing that prompted us to celebrate birthdays. It used to be that which allowed us to get a driver's license, a marriage license, a business license. Aging once was our ticket to freedom. But in the winter of life, it ceases to free us and begins to confine us.

I have contemplated these things recently as I've watched my grandmother's mind and body fail. Why do we have to deal with such injury and insult? From the beginning of time, aging has done this to every human being (with a few biblical exceptions). It has brought us to our deathbeds and then left us there, alone, abandoned. Why does this seem so odd to me if its always been this way? Maybe because it wasn't supposed to be this way!

When God created the Garden of Eden, He made no provision for death within its lush surroundings. That's right, Eden had no nursing home and no cemetery. There was no thought of Adam ordering from the senior menu or Eve getting an AARP card in the mail. Cans of Ensure or boxes of Depends never landed in their shopping carts.

The fact is, we weren't created to die. Alzheimer's, Parkinson's, cancer, and heart disease were never a part of the original owner's manual—not even in fine print in the back.

Death was an intruder in the Garden. An *invited* intruder, perhaps, but a trespasser nonetheless.

The betrayal of age and the onset of death will always seem counterintuitive because they are counter-creation. God created us to be uncorrupted by sin, untouched by death. But when sin entered the garden, death entered our race.

Death...and something else—redemption.

Even as God was pronouncing judgment and death in the book of Genesis, He was looking ahead through the years at our rescue, redemption, and eternal life. Strange that such a promise would come in words spoken to a serpent!

> I will put enmity
>> between you and the woman,
>> and between your offspring and hers;
> he will crush your head,
>> and you will strike his heel (Genesis 3:15).

In the fullness of time, Jesus was that Offspring of the woman who crushed the serpent's head. In His days on earth, He would boldly proclaim, "A thief is only there to steal and kill and destroy. I came so they can have real and eternal life, more and better life than they ever dreamed of" (John 10:10 MSG).

He is the resurrection and the life, and anyone who believes in Him will never die but will instead have the light of life. So when aging brings us to the doorstep of the undertaker, it should feel odd—and make us long for heaven. That's because we weren't made for time; we were made for eternity.

My friend Larry's father lived into his nineties. Shortly before the older man's passing, Larry described how his dad would sit and stare at the back of his thin, bony hands with their protruding veins. It was almost as if couldn't believe what he was seeing. How had he come to be so old, so frail? How and when did it happen? How curious it seemed!

The fact is, you and I weren't designed for death; we were wired for life.

As I contemplate my precious grandmother's passing this week, I shed tears of loss, tears of remembrance, and tears of gratitude. But they are also tears shed in recognition of our collective loss. Tears that confirm that Eden had no tombstones. Tears proclaiming that life, not death, is our ultimate reality.

So it seems to me that to taste our mortality is to realize that maybe aging really is our friend after all. At the end of the day, aging doesn't deceive us and abandon us to death, it introduces us to truth and life.

For while we are in this tent, we groan and are
burdened, because we do not wish to be unclothed
but to be clothed with our heavenly dwelling, so that
what is mortal may be swallowed up by life. Now
it is God who has made us for this very purpose and
has given us the Spirit as a deposit, guaranteeing
what is to come (2 Corinthians 5:4-5).

What's Percolating in Me: My Response

_____

_____

_____

_____

Spill the Beans: My Prayer

_____

_____

_____

_____

Thanks a Latte! My Praise

_____

_____

_____

_____

ON OUR FLIGHT FROM TULSA TO DALLAS, some unique passengers joined us. His name was Pete, her name was Penny. And their last name was Penguin.

As my friend Melinda and I checked in, we did so with the penguins and their accompanying humans. They were from Sea World in San Antonio and were returning from a multiple-city goodwill tour, where they visited children's hospitals. The ticket agent ushered Melinda and me, along with the penguins, to the hallway, where we waited to board the plane. If you are blind (or if you're a penguin), you get to board earlier than the sighted human passengers.

As we waited, we began to question the trainer as to penguin protocol.

After a comfort level was established, I asked the trainer if he would mind our taking a picture of the penguins so we could show our children. He was very accommodating and offered for us to kneel next to the crates where Pete and Penny traveled.

As we knelt, much to our surprise, the handler opened the crates and placed Pete on my lap and Penny on the lap of my friend.

We were astonished. It was the most amazing experience to touch a little ten-pound penguin named Pete. He waddled around for us in his little tuxedo as if he knew he had an adoring audience.

Once we boarded, the flight attendant announced that Pete and Penny would take a customary walk down the aisle of the aircraft.

The crowd extended a collective sigh of fascination as the penguin couple weebled and wobbled like two little married people trying to find their seats, all the while squawking at each other. I laughingly told Melinda, "That's Phil and me in 50 years."

We were all taught in grade school that penguins can't fly. Well, Pete and Penny did. When I think of the penguins, I'm reminded that right in the middle of ordinary days, sometimes God interrupts with just a breath of magic. Sometimes He lets us hear music that causes our hearts to skip a beat, or He gives us a Pete-and-Penny moment with a reason to laugh—one of those big laughs that makes our eyes water.

What an amazing God, who created those two little toddlers in tuxedos. And what an amazing God, who interrupted my ordinary day with such an extraordinary enchantment.

Expect your extraordinary God to interrupt your ordinary day with a glimpse of His wonder today. And, my friend, tune in! Open the eyes of faith and look for His shadow on your sidewalk; listen for His voice in the chatter of a crowd. He wants to enchant you with who He is today.

Invite Him to do just that.

O Lord, how many are Your works!
In wisdom You have made them all;
The earth is full of Your possessions
(Psalm 104:24 NASB).

What's Percolating in Me: My Response

_____

_____

_____

_____

Spill the Beans: My Prayer

_____

_____

_____

_____

Thanks a Latte! My Praise

_____

_____

_____

_____

56

The Privilege
of Forgiveness

HAVE YOU EVER BECOME FRIENDS with someone you've never met? I have, and his name is Nathaniel Hawthorne. Even though I was born nearly a century after his death, I have come to know him by his books—most recently, *The Scarlet Letter*.

I know I must have read that volume in high school, but at the time, I guess Leif Garrett and Shaun Cassidy were just more interesting to me than Hester Prynne, Roger Chillingworth, and Authur Dimmesdale. But as Robertson Davies says, "A truly great book should be read in youth, again in maturity, and once more in old age, as a fine building should be seen by morning light, at noon, and by moonlight."

Well, I'm not sure if I am in the noontime of my life or heading into early evening, but I do know I'm crazy about how Hawthorne has introduced me to many life-changing truths about myself and my God.

Recently, I was struck by the way Hawthorne handles the subject of hate. Maybe it's the condition of our world that made the topic rise to the surface as I read. Or maybe it's just the unredeemed condition of our hearts that caused me to recognize the familiar darkness in one of the book's characters.

Old Roger Chillingworth was the scorned husband of Hester Prynne. He carried out a secret strategy to violate his wife's lover as deeply as he, himself, had been violated. He finds himself playing the role of the devil and comes to realize that his hate is transforming him. At one point in the story, with utter shock and disdain, he looks and fully sees who he has become because of his hatred. He had sought to repay, and he was the one who paid.

Hate shrivels our souls and turns us into an object more distasteful than that which we abhor in the first place.

The main character, Hester, sees the terrible toll that hate, revenge, guilt, and secrecy are taking on each of them. She pleads with Chillingworth to stop torturing her former lover, Arthur Dimmesdale. Of course, the obsessed Chillingworth refuses. In desperation, Hester asks if Dimmesdale's suffering served to pay his debt to him.

Chillingworth responds, "No, his debt has only increased."

What a graphic portrayal of hate and revenge; truly, they are never satisfied. The urge only grows. The cancer only metastasizes.

Hester is able to see that the only one who can free Chillingworth from this "evil maze" is himself. She pleads for him to forgive, to unchain both himself and Dimmesdale.

"There might be good for thee, and thee alone, since thou hast been deeply wronged and hast it at thy will to pardon. Wilt thou give up that only privilege? Wilt thou reject that priceless benefit?"

Have you ever thought of pardon as a privilege and forgiveness as a priceless benefit? Hawthorne did. (Do you see why I like him so much?)

Forgiveness alone quenches the thirsty flame of hate. Only love satisfies the need for revenge. God is more familiar with our frail human condition than we are, so He reminds us over and over again that vengeance belongs to Him. Our role is not to exact revenge, but instead to exercise forgiveness.

I once heard Bill Bright say that what you feed grows, and what you starve dies. So with that in mind, let's starve the life of hatred and feed love, tolerance, and forgiveness so that they blossom and grow.

Imagine living in a neighborhood where your next-door neighbor allowed his house to deteriorate, never cut his lawn or pulled the weeds, and allowed trash to build up on the property. That happened to my friend's elderly mother. Although she tried her best to keep her own property looking nice in this older neighborhood, her neighbor's house was a complete wreck. The city wouldn't do anything about the situation, so the lady took matters into her own hands and planted flowering vines along the chain-link fence separating the properties.

Now she can sit in her little backyard, and instead of looking at an eyesore, she sees greenery and flowers.

Feed love and forgiveness, my friend, and they will grow, blossom, and cover a multitude of sins. Don't neglect the privilege of pardon!

The punishment inflicted on him by the majority is
sufficient for him. Now instead, you ought to forgive
and comfort him, so that he will not be overwhelmed
by excessive sorrow (2 Corinthians 2:6-7).

What's Percolating in Me: My Response

_____

_____

_____

_____

Spill the Beans: My Prayer

_____

_____

_____

_____

Thanks a Latte! My Praise

_____

_____

_____

_____

57

Memories
of Heaven

FROM A DEATHBED IN BETHANY, Lazarus was ushered into God's presence.

It had to have been the most elating, magnificent moment of his life. Nothing in all his years of walking the earth could remotely compare with that overpowering moment when he stepped out of his weak, painful mortality and entered ultimate strength, soaring beauty, and unlimited joy in the presence of his God.

That was *not*, however, what his loving sisters had been praying for.

For days, Mary and Martha nursed him, prayed to Jehovah, and even summoned Jesus to come help. After all, if Jesus were there, surely their brother wouldn't die. But Jesus didn't come in time, and Lazarus slipped away from his mortal body.

The mourners arrived, and finally, so did Jesus.

So while all his relatives and friends wept at his tomb, what was the scene for Lazarus? For days now (if we count days in heaven), he had mingled with angels, talked to prophets, and laughed with departed loved ones and childhood friends. And he had worshipped. Oh, how he had worshipped the great King. He was healed, whole, and home.

And then (remember that "Ctrl-Z" button I wrote about?) a Voice spoke before the tomb, somewhere back on faraway planet Earth. It was the Voice the angels had heard as an infant cry in Bethlehem decades before and the Voice that would soon cry in agony, "It is finished" from a Roman cross. It was the Voice, the Word, that had spoken creation itself into existence.

And now, the Voice called Lazarus back.

He must have known to whom it belonged. He had listened to the Voice weave stories about the kingdom of God during long, lingering suppers. Though in that moment the Voice sounded more authoritative, he knew it was Jesus, for "his sheep follow him because they know his voice."

Lazarus obeyed the Voice that beckoned him, "Come out!" And come out he did. Stepping out of some scene of heart-melting beauty, emerging from the depths of an ocean of peace and joy, he returned to his old body and was again clothed with corruptible flesh.

Certainly his sisters' prayers were answered. They beheld their brother with their eyes and held him in their arms. What they loved and lost was returned. But what about Lazarus? He returned to earth just to someday encounter the same sorrowful fate. He would again feel the pangs of death wrack his deteriorating body. He would again leave his brokenness and enter into wholeness, be embraced by the angels with whom he would once more worship, and fall again before the throne.

I wonder what secret longings Lazarus harbored as the years of his renewed earthly life slipped by? Did he find himself homesick for some of those little corners of Glory he could still remember? Did certain celestial images still burn with the fires of longing in his memory? As he caught the aroma of one of Martha's best culinary creations, did it spark a memory of feeding from the tree of life? When he complimented his sister on some "heavenly" dish from her kitchen, did he mean exactly that?

Who really benefited from Lazarus' return? The women were destined to cry again, and Lazarus was destined to die again.

Thinking through this story made me wonder…for whose benefit do I pray? I'll bet Mary and Martha prayed from the depths for Lazarus not to die—and then prayed with the same fervency for him to return.

Who wouldn't? When someone we love is sick or dies, we just want God to deliver us from our pain. But for Mary and Martha to gain, Lazarus had to lose. For their pain to cease, his pain had to return. It just makes me rethink the way I pray. Instead of praying so that I gain, I want to pray more thoroughly—for the good and merciful will of God for all of us.

I get lots of e-mails that ask me to pray for precious people with terminal illnesses. And I do! I pray with full faith and fervent compassion. I just don't want to pray under the faulty assumption that continuing life on earth is the best answer to my prayer. As hard as it is to say, mercy takes precious people to heaven even when we plead for them to stay right where they are. And when that happens, we need to think of Lazarus and remember that it's okay for us to lose in order for someone whom we deeply love to ultimately gain.

I am torn between the two: I desire to
depart and be with Christ, which is
better by far (Philippians 1:23).

What's Percolating in Me: My Response

_____

_____

_____

_____

Spill the Beans: My Prayer

_____

_____

_____

_____

Thanks a Latte! My Praise

_____

_____

_____

_____

58

Gift Anxiety

AS I TYPE THESE WORDS, only 70 more shopping days remain until Christmas.

Maybe that bit of information doesn't move you at all.

Then again, perhaps you feel a slight tingle of excitement as you contemplate malls, mistletoe, and chestnuts roasting. (Does anybody really roast chestnuts on an open fire anymore?) Or maybe this bit of news is meaningless to you because you've been shopping clearance racks and closeouts all year long. You're so amazingly efficient and organized that your holiday shopping was done by Labor Day.

Or perhaps you're like me, and this little reminder has the potential of *alarming* you. Yes, I am already starting to feel the onset of a slow-building, long-lasting anxiety attack.

As much as I love our Christmas celebrations, buying gifts can sometimes send me into an emotional and mental tailspin. It's not spending the money that causes my psychological pain— no, it's the mostly self-imposed pressure of purchasing the perfect present. Yes, I have a rare condition called *gift anxiety.*

Will he like it?

Does she already have one?

If this blouse is too big, will she think I think she's fat?

Smile if you like, but these are the questions that haunt me.

I'm afflicted with buyer's remorse before I've even bought anything. And after I do make the purchase, it just gets worse. I know, the sane thing would be to buy those nifty gift cards you can use like credit cards at all those wonderful establishments. Believe me, I've done that. Then the voices whisper, *They'll think you didn't take time to shop for them! How impersonal.*

You see, gift anxiety is serious. During certain seasons it's practically debilitating. Why can't I be a good gift giver? You know, the one who always provokes oohs and aahs, the one who always hears, "That's just what I wanted!"

Well, I may just need to medicate my condition with candy canes and eggnog and focus on the One who does give good gifts.

James tells us that every good and perfect gift comes down from our heavenly Father. But I'm sure He doesn't always hear oohs and aahs from us, or "That's just what I wanted." Some of God's gifts come in packages we didn't expect. Some of His good and perfect gifts are discovered deep within the wrappings of heartache and disappointment.

Sometimes He gifts us with what we need, rather than what we want—and we don't discover until later how His gifts really did perfect us and work goodness in our lives.

I don't ever want God to feel gift anxiety over what He lovingly chooses to send my way. I want Him to be blessed in knowing that I won't complain or be cranky, but rather receive, unwrap, discover, and simply say, "Thank You, Lord. This must be just what I needed."

How do you receive what God allows in your life? Are you grateful? Do you trust that He knows just what you need—even if it's not what you wanted? My friend, His ways, His timing, and His gifts are perfect. Trust and thank Him.

> *Every good thing given and every perfect*
> *gift is from above, coming down from the*
> *Father of lights (James 1:17 NASB).*

❧

What's Percolating in Me: My Response

_____

_____

_____

Spill the Beans: My Prayer

_____

_____

_____

Thanks a Latte! My Praise

_____

_____

_____

59

In His Hands

As a 15-year-old girl, one of the first songs I wrote was called "In His Hands." I would sit at my living room piano and sing the lyrics with full earnest and belief. I was confident to sing in those early days only when no one else was listening, so my only audience was God. A simple lyric from the song that I can still remember is "I don't know what tomorrow holds, but I know it's in His hands."

In His hands may be a commonly used phrase, but as I go through life, I have found that it is an uncommon way to live. To live in His hands is to live in utter dependence upon God, with an intimate understanding of His moment-by-moment presence.

My friend Stephanie Wright lived in His hands.

Stephanie was an event coordinator for LifeWay Christian Resources in Nashville. She specialized in women's events and helped to pull off the massive Beth Moore Living Proof weekends. I first met Stephanie at a national LifeWay women's conference, where I had been invited to speak. Over the years, we have met at numerous meetings, conferences, and conventions.

Beyond her always sweet disposition, what always struck me most about Stephanie was her peacefulness. You don't have to see a woman with physical eyes to sense someone who is at peace with herself, and it's a quality I find very attractive. A few summers ago, Stephanie drove me back to the airport after a meeting, and once again, I marveled to her that I could not believe a man hadn't snagged her yet.

Thirty-one and single, Stephanie laughed and responded, as she had in the past, that she was content with Jesus and knew He would provide the perfect marriage when it was time.

Such an occasion came on December 23 of that year. On her way home for the Christmas holiday, Stephanie was involved in a horrible car accident. Stephanie, who lived her life in His hands, died in those same hands. She was instantly united with the Man of her dreams. As part of the bride of Christ, she was welcomed into His arms.

I'll bet she recognized Him by His lovely hands. For those were the hands that held her, guided her, protected her, and comforted her through this life.

A Christmas letter she mailed out before her accident made reference to those hands of Christ. I want to leave those words with you as an encouragement to live as she did.

> I pray that you will allow God to continue the work He began in you this past weekend. He WILL be faithful to complete it. I pray you have a merry Christmas and a happy new year. Enjoy time with your family and friends remembering why we celebrate. God sent His only Son for us so we might have relationship with Him. May we never take that for granted. May we count everything else as loss just to know Him. God bless you

all, and we will look forward to seeing you next
year. In His hands…

Stephanie Wright

In His hands is far more than a simple song lyric; it's a lifestyle.
We really don't know what tomorrow holds, but we do know that
it is in His hands. Let's live as if we really know and believe that.
May each of us live in His hands, and in the words of Stephanie,
may we count everything else as loss just to know Him.

> *But I trust in you, O LORD;*
> *I say, "You are my God."*
> *My times are in your hands (Psalm 31:14-15).*

༄

🫘 What's Percolating in Me: My Response

_____

_____

🫘 Spill the Beans: My Prayer

_____

_____

🫘 Thanks a Latte! My Praise

_____

_____

60

The Story
Behind the Song

THE FACT THAT HORATIO SPAFFORD could pen the words "It is well with my soul" is truly amazing when you understand that it was *not* well with his circumstances.

In fact, it had not been well for many years.

Horatio Spafford was a successful Chicago lawyer who had invested heavily in real estate. In the Great Chicago Fire in October 1871, the Spaffords lost almost everything they owned. This occurred even as Horatio and his wife were still grieving the death of their son, who had died earlier that same dreadful year.

Two years later, in 1873, Horatio's friend D.L. Moody was holding evangelistic crusades in England. Spafford felt that his family needed a break from the sadness and decided to take them on a holiday in Europe to see their friend. Sending his wife and four daughters—Tanetta, Maggie, Annie, and Bessie—ahead, he planned to join them as soon as he had wrapped up some business dealings.

On November 21, 1873, while crossing the Atlantic, the ship carrying Spafford's wife and children was struck by an iron sailing vessel. On that dark day, 226 people lost their lives, including all four of Spafford's daughters. His wife, Anna, was reportedly found floating unconscious on a piece of the ship's mast. When she and the remaining survivors arrived in England, she sent a telegram to Horatio containing these profound words: "Saved alone."

Can you imagine his heartbreak? First the death of his son, then the loss of personal wealth and business, and then the deaths of four beloved daughters. The human soul can absorb only so much sorrow.

It was not well with his circumstances.

According to Bertha Spafford (a daughter born later to Horatio and Anna), Spafford boarded a ship to go to England to meet his grief-stricken wife. As he sailed past the place where his daughters died, he penned the moving words that we now know as "It Is Well with My Soul."

> When peace like a river attendeth my way,
> When sorrows like sea billows roll;
> Whatever my lot, Thou hast taught me to say,
> "It is well, it is well with my soul."
>
> Though Satan should buffet, though trials
> should come,
> Let this blest assurance control,
> That Christ hath regarded my helpless estate,
> And hath shed His own blood for my soul.
>
> My sin, oh, the bliss of this glorious thought!
> My sin, not in part but the whole,
> Is nailed to the cross, and I bear it no more,
> Praise the Lord, praise the Lord, O my soul!

And Lord, haste the day when the faith shall
be sight,
The clouds be rolled back as a scroll;
The trump shall resound, and the Lord
shall descend,
Even so, it is well with my soul.

So, next time you stand to sing that beloved hymn in church, remember that it doesn't have to be well with your circumstances for it to be well with your soul.

When my spirit grows faint within me,
it is you who know my way (Psalm 142:3).

❧

🍂 What's Percolating in Me: My Response

_____

_____

🍂 Spill the Beans: My Prayer

_____

_____

🍂 Thanks a Latte! My Praise

_____

_____

Janatude

"WHAT I AM GOING TO TAKE away is Janatude."

These were the words of Jana's sister at her funeral. Jana was a lovely woman of many graces. She was a mother of two sons, the youngest of which is autistic. She and her husband, John, had been part of our small group Bible study for years, and I always loved hearing her chime in with her opinion during class. She offered tender, thoughtful, and tested words to the discussion.

Jana knew God and loved Him. Her diabetes and epilepsy—combined with her son's autism—had paved a path that took her deep into the heart of God. And it showed.

I frequently told her she was smart. And when I did, her response was always the same. "Naw, I'm just opinionated."

Jana passed away in her sleep one night not long ago, leaving a gaping hole in the fabric of our church, her home, and the hearts of all who knew her.

But what remains is Janatude.

That was Jana's incomparable blend of optimism, wit, and faith that she brought to everyone and every situation.

If she'd been looking for such, Jana had plenty of reasons to get discouraged. Instead, she always offered encouragement. That's Janatude. She should have spent lots of time crying, but she smiled more than she frowned. That's Janatude. She could have been hopeless about the future, but she faced it with vigor and eagerness. That's Janatude.

To be honest, I really can't believe she's gone. I will miss her spunk. But I too will put on some of her Janatude. What a special gift to leave behind to those who remain—an attitude worth emulating.

As we drove home from the funeral, I wondered, *What attitude will I be remembered for? Is there a Jennitude? And what does that look like?*

What attitude will you be remembered for? Winston Churchill once said, "Attitude is a little thing that makes a big difference."

What we say is seldom remembered. What we do is often forgotten. But people notice the attitude with which we say and do things in this life. A person's attitude and spirit show his or her character most clearly.

We can't disguise our attitudes with our actions or hide it with our words, for our attitude cuts through the clamor of our activity and words, revealing our true selves.

Earl Nightingale spoke truly when he said, "Our attitude toward life determines life's attitude toward us." Attitudes are contagious, so may you and I infect all we know with a Janatude. May we be the bearers of attitudes that reveal a life changed and shaped by Christ.

> *Let Christ himself be your example as to what your attitude should be (Philippians 2:5 PHILLIPS).*

What's Percolating in Me: My Response

_____

_____

_____

_____

Spill the Beans: My Prayer

_____

_____

_____

_____

Thanks a Latte! My Praise

_____

_____

_____

_____

62

Learning to Bend

OUR OLDEST, CLAYTON, has now had two violin lessons.

He goes with his dad each Thursday night for 30 minutes of tutelage. But last Thursday they didn't come back promptly after the lesson—they were a whole hour late.

Finally, I heard the garage door open. Because I was in our youngest son's room at the end of the house, I could barely hear them as they came in—muffled voices, trailing footsteps, and bulky jackets were all I could detect. I expected them to call for me and Connor and then come down the hall toward Connor's room, but they didn't. Instead, I heard their bulky procession lumbering down our stairs into the basement.

What are they doing? I thought. *It's not like them to not say hello.*

Finally, my curiosity catapulted me downstairs and I blurted out as I entered the basement, "What are you guys up to?"

"Honey, I bought a recliner," Phil proudly announced.

"You did?" I shot back with disbelief. Phil and I have been shopping for a recliner for several years, but our priorities haven't exactly been the same. For Phil, comfort trumps appearance hands down. I, on the other hand, wanted something that would fit in with the décor. He wanted the perfect feel; I wanted the perfect fabric. As a result, we hadn't been able to decide on anything.

Until now.

After my disbelief began to wear off, I felt a little relief. *He knows what we've been looking for, and he must have found it—the perfect recliner to match the old-world décor in the basement. Yes,* I thought, *just in time for the holidays—we've got our recliner.*

"So what does it look like?" I asked.

He hesitated. I didn't really care for that hesitation.

"Well," he finally said, "it's black."

At that point, my relief was turning to panic *"Black?* Black isn't a color that matches our other furniture, Phil," I said with as much control as possible.

"I know," he said. "But it's so *comfortable.* It heats up and massages you."

By now, I had made my way over to the new chair. I shrieked as I ran my hand over the sleek, space-age combination of metal and leather that someone actually had the nerve to call a recliner. It looked more like the pilot's chair in the space shuttle. Or maybe a reclining dental chair. Let's just say my basement now looked like "Sharper Image meets Old World."

I didn't like it at all. Not at all.

I thought it was distasteful at best and hideous at worst, but Phil loved it. And so I went upstairs (where the furnishings were warm, homey, planned, and inviting) and began to ponder.

What's more important, my desire for the house to look a certain way or Phil's happiness over the ugly chair? Flexible is not usually a quality attributed to my type-A personality, but I began to bend. How much, in the whole scheme of things, did one mismatched, unattractive chair really matter to me? Not nearly as much as my goofy husband matters to me. So I'm trying to fix my eyes on what matters, focus on what counts, and bend, bend, bend.

Besides, if Mr. Spock of the old Star Trek series ever beams into our downstairs with a sore back, he'll feel right at home in Phil's new antigravity vibrating chair.

So girls, whatever seems to be distracting, annoying, or just plain ugly in your life, try to see right through it and fix your eyes on what really matters. After all, the apostle Paul was right: What is seen truly is temporary.

> *So we fix our eyes not on what is seen, but on what is unseen. For what is seen is temporary, but what is unseen is eternal (2 Corinthians 4:18).*

What's Percolating in Me: My Response

Spill the Beans: My Prayer

Thanks a Latte! My Praise

63

Like a River Glorious

My home was unusually quiet because I was alone.

Alone…

That can be a wonderful state of affairs when you hardly ever experience it. I'm sure it wouldn't hold such appeal if it was an all-the-time circumstance. But if you knew what it was like at my house on most days, you'd know why *alone* and *quiet* are words seldom used to describe my pilgrimage on earth.

Trying to adjust to the unaccustomed solitude, I wandered aimlessly about the house for 15 minutes or so. Not surprisingly, my wandering eventually led me to the piano bench, where I sat down and began to play. The soft melodies resonated throughout my living room and with each note, sweet memories began to dance through my mind.

I played "'Tis So Sweet to Trust in Jesus" and thought of a time when Phil and I were newlyweds. I played, "When the Night Is Falling" by Dennis Jernigan and thought of my precious friend Thierry, who had gone to heaven. Then I began to play a song I hadn't played in years. It was an old hymn my mother taught me.

The hymn was "Like a River Glorious." Do you remember those grand, flowing words?

> Like a river glorious is God's perfect peace,
> Over all victorious in its bright increase;
> Perfect, yet it floweth fuller ev'ry day,
> Perfect, yet it groweth deeper all the way.
>
> Stayed upon Jehovah, hearts are fully blest,
> Finding, as He promised, perfect peace and rest.
>
> Ev'ry joy or trial falleth from above,
> Traced upon our dial by the Sun of Love;
> We may trust Him fully, all for us to do.
> They who trust Him wholly find Him wholly true.

As I played each note, I was drawn to a memory of my mom. Each Sunday night, my church hosted a "favorite hymn" time. "Like a River Glorious" was the hymn my mom requested most often. I used to love standing next to her as we sang. Her beautiful alto voice was as rich and tender as her own soul. As my fingers pressed each key, I realized that if I could see my hands on the keyboard, I would probably recognize hands that looked much like my mom's.

You see, when I recall standing next to her and harmonizing on those Sunday nights so many years ago, she was just a few years younger than I am now.

When my mom was in her late thirties, she had a daughter who was in the early stages of blindness. My mother had a heartbreak I can't ever really wrap my mind around. She carried a heavy, unsolicited burden with grace, tenacity, and even peace.

Somehow, she knew something of that glorious river that flowed through the arid places of her soul. She had tasted the living water that quenched her thirst for answers. She drank from its sweetness, and it washed away the bitter sting of darkness. I think my mom understood something about wholly trusting, and I know she found her God to be wholly true.

I want the beauty of this hymn not only to fill my living room—I want the music of its truth to fill my life. I long to live out the legacy and lyrics of my mother's life. For I am the daughter who is now almost fully blind, yet I can see perfectly the river about which she sang.

It is the river of peace that she led me to through the example of her faithful life.

If you and I, like my mom, trust Him wholly, we will find Him wholly true. There's plenty of water in that river of peace, my friend, so let it wash over you today and fill you. And then may its living water spill out of your faithful life.

I will give of the fountain of the water of life freely to him who thirsts (Revelation 21:6 NKJV).

What's Percolating in Me: My Response

_____

_____

_____

_____

Spill the Beans: My Prayer

_____

_____

_____

_____

Thanks a Latte! My Praise

_____

_____

_____

_____

64

Lost and Found

AS A THIRD GRADER, Clayton was obsessed with a highly coveted, very expensive, and pretty nifty yo-yo. He had asked for this particular device since he turned nine that year. His dad and I avoided the big purchase originally because we thought the yo-yo fad would quickly fizzle. When it didn't, we were presented with a whole new dilemma: The yo-yo he wanted cost $40.

Yikes. This was no ordinary yo-yo. It had wooden ball bearings and a seven-minute sleep time, and it was a Bumble Bee—the yo-yo of the pros. So in order to justify such an extravagant purchase, we attached the valuable prize to a highly valued accomplishment. Good grades.

I scrimped and saved, putting aside money for my son's desired treasure. I researched, shopped, and even searched for used yo-yos that would be acceptable. But in the end, of course, only a brand-new official Bumble Bee would do.

So when the report card arrived, we took the straight-A boy to the mall and reluctantly relinquished our $40. Now, before you think we were cheap or hesitant without reason, let me explain.

Our family had just moved that summer to Springfield, Missouri, and moving is expensive. It just wasn't the easiest summer to part with $40. We knew how much it was costing us. But he had worked hard and earned it, and to be there to experience his utter joy as he became the proud owner was worth every penny.

A week after the big yo-yo purchase, we shopped the mall for some home furnishings. Clayton carried his new Bumble Bee in his pocket, occasionally pulling it out to "walk the dog" or go "around the world." He was really enjoying it. But after a few hours and a few stops, a panicked little voice exclaimed, "My yo-yo! It's *gone!*"

We retraced our steps, asked clerks in the stores where we'd shopped if they'd seen the missing yo-yo, and grew more and more discouraged as we searched.

"I know someone took it." Clay was convinced, and I feared he was right. Even a yo-yo ignoramus could recognize that this yo-yo didn't come from the dollar store. Now he was heartbroken, and I was even more frustrated about the $40 price tag.

Just then, Phil suggested we check back at the store where we had purchased the yo-yo. Clay and I protested because more than a week had passed since we'd made the purchase. We hadn't even walked by that store on this shopping venture.

"Well, you never know," Phil said. "Someone might have turned it in to them." Clay and I doubted it, but we trudged to the yo-yo kiosk anyway.

When we arrived, I told the salesman the sad saga. He promptly went behind the counter and pulled out Clayton's yo-yo, explaining that someone had indeed brought it to his store.

I could hear Clayton's quiet gasp. I, on the other hand, could barely contain my excitement. I broke into song. "Praise God from whom all blessings flow!"

I was rejoicing loudly and celebrating without a care of my

audience. The sales guy just offered an awkward "yeah," and Clayton was pretty quiet…I think he was a little embarrassed by his fanatical mom.

I rejoiced the loudest because the yo-yo had cost me the most. I knew its value, so I understood that its return was worth a celebration. I knew the sacrifice that was required to acquire it in the first place, so I knew it was worth a party to celebrate its return.

In Luke 15, Jesus tells the grumbling Pharisees about some lost things that were found, and the return of each one caused an all-out party.

When the shepherd found his lost sheep, when the woman located her lost coin, and when the father received back his lost son, it was party, party, party. Jesus told the crowd gathered in Capernaum that in the same way there is rejoicing in heaven over the lost being found.

You are that one lost sheep. You are so valuable to the Good Shepherd that He pursues you, scoops you up into His arms, and rejoices. In other words, you are worth throwing a party for. For centuries the halls of heaven have resonated with the sound of great rejoicing each time a lost one has come home.

Don't ever underestimate whose rejoicing is the loudest in heaven. I'm sure the angels blow their trumpets and exclaim, "Hallelujah!" I can almost hear the saints that have gone before clapping, cheering, and praising. But I think there is probably one voice that is heard above the gleeful exaltation.

Surely one voice thunders and exalts the loudest. It must be the voice of Father God leading the chorus of joy. After all, He truly understands the cost. He truly recognizes your incredible worth. My friend, He loves you.

In the same way, there is more joy in heaven over one lost sinner who repents and returns to God than over ninety-nine others who are righteous and haven't strayed away! (Luke 15:7 NLT).

❧

What's Percolating in Me: My Response

_____

_____

_____

Spill the Beans: My Prayer

_____

_____

_____

Thanks a Latte! My Praise

_____

_____

_____

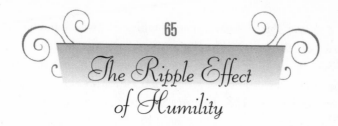

65

The Ripple Effect
of Humility

DURING THE REVOLUTIONARY WAR, Aaron Burr returned to New York from a failed assault on Quebec—with no apparent damage to his standing and reputation.

Colonel Burr enjoyed a great reputation at that point in history. General Washington honored him with an invitation to serve on his military staff, or "family," as it was fondly referred to in that day. With grandiose expectations, the aristocratic Colonel Burr accepted General Washington's invitation.

Burr reportedly imagined Washington would consult him on great matters of strategy in regard to the war against England, but that didn't seem to be in the cards. Once Colonel Burr realized he would be relegated to more colorless and commonplace duties, his puffed-up plan slowly deflated. With indignation and injured pride, he decided to quit, burning General Washington on his exit with a scathing letter of protest.

History tells us that Burr fumed over the fact that "less qualified" men than he had been granted promotion. Most likely, Burr's political future had been shaped by his wartime relationship with Washington. Burr's contemporaries, like Alexander Hamilton, benefited greatly from Washington's esteem.

Aaron Burr, however, began taking steps on a pugnacious path of self-promotion and political posturing—at any cost. In 1804, while Burr was vice president under Thomas Jefferson, he ran for the position of governor of New York. He lost, blaming the defeat on U.S. Treasury Secretary Alexander Hamilton. Claiming Hamilton had smeared his name, he challenged the secretary to a duel. Such challenges rarely led to violence, but in this case, Burr actually killed Hamilton in a shameful encounter in Weehawken, New Jersey.

Fleeing to Washington DC, Burr avoided prosecution, but President Jefferson discarded him as a running mate that year. Soon after that, Burr tried to seize part of Louisiana (which was then a huge region that Jefferson had purchased from Napoleon) and turn it into an independent country. History has even proven that Burr had the intention of annexing Texas and much of the West to form his own empire. Foiled in his attempt, Burr was tried for treason but acquitted on a technicality.

Burr was willing to do whatever was necessary to promote himself and maintain his pride. The eventual cost was the frown of history on this great-grandson of the respected preacher Jonathan Edwards.

Aaron Burr was full of himself. Lacking perspective and anything approaching respectful deference, he stoked a lifelong appetite of schemes and deception. What a shame. Pride cometh before a fall.

Now, here's my question. What if Aaron Burr had been humble? What if his greatest passion had been love for country rather than love of prestige and pleasure? What if he had been more concerned with self-sacrifice than with self-promotion? How would his life have been different? How would American history have been different?

That question leads me to an even more important question. What if *I* am truly humble? How will my personal history be different? How will my future and the future of those I influence be different? What if my greatest concern is self-sacrifice rather than self-preservation?

To think that our own pride or humility can have such a powerful rippling effect is compelling. We must consider the cost of our own self-promotion. Are we incurring debt that we will forever pay and leave our posterity to assume? Is pride really worth its cost? How valuable is humility?

Pride costs too much. Humility gives much more than it takes, and it broadens a person more than it limits. The warm glow of history illuminates the humble life because the result of humility is reflected in the countless lives it touches.

Before his downfall a man's heart is proud,
but humility comes before honor (Proverbs 18:12).

What's Percolating in Me: My Response

_____

_____

_____

_____

Spill the Beans: My Prayer

_____

_____

_____

_____

Thanks a Latte! My Praise

_____

_____

_____

_____

66

The Three-Week Rule

EACH SUNDAY I LOYALLY FOLLOW the three-week rule. You know, if you sit on the same church pew three weeks in a row, its yours.

It's as if an invisible placard reserves your seat each Sunday. No other people would ever think of sitting there. After all, they too are probably loyally following the three-week rule and growing roots beneath their own designated seats.

The three-week rule gives us a great way to identify visitors. Everyone in the church can spot the newcomers as they survey the sanctuary and then veer toward an empty pew. The novices innocently plop down in someone else's pew because they can't read the invisible No Sit Zone placard.

You can almost hear the onlookers whisper as the unsuspecting guests take the secretly reserved seats. "Oh, no. Someone's sitting in Frank and Ethel's seats...what in the world will they do? Where will they sit? If Frank and Ethel have to sit somewhere else, they'll take another faithful parishioner's assigned seats. The church as we know it will never be the same."

Okay, I'm exaggerating. But the point I am about to make is not what you might think. I'm not really opposed to following the three-week rule. There's something to be said for sitting in the same pew, with the same people, at the same church, Sunday after Sunday. It helps build community and deepen relationships.

I, for example, sit on the second pew with the Eldridge family. After three weeks of sitting there, I grafted myself in. Mr. Eldridge was diagnosed with cancer several months ago, and his prognosis isn't good. The doctors say his days remaining here on earth are in the double digits.

As I seek the Lord next to that faithful family, my worship has become more meaningful. As I sing of heaven, I imagine my dear old friend celebrating there before the year ends. As I praise God for His faithfulness, my mind travels down the pew to dear Mr. Eldridge, and I try to hear his voice as he sings of God's faithfulness. I suspect he understands God's faithfulness in a much deeper way these days.

How I long each Sunday to sit with that family, whom I love, respect, and pray for.

This past Sunday, however, was Mother's Day, and a lot of people unfamiliar with the three-week rule attended our services. (Can you imagine?) And yes, they encroached upon my staked-out territory with the Eldridges.

I ended up sitting back a few rows with Betsy—one of our college students. As the pastor asked the moms in the congregation to rise, I was painfully aware that Betsy had lost her mom several years earlier, and I began to pray for that sweet young woman. As we sang about God's faithfulness again, I tried to hear Betsy's voice, for she knows about God's faithfulness in a way and in an area of life that I haven't yet experienced. As we praised God for His provision, my mind wandered down the pew to Betsy, for I know He has lovingly provided for her during days of pain and loss.

After the service, I took her hand and asked if Mother's Day had been difficult for her.

She responded with surprise. "You remembered?"

"Of course I remembered," I said as our eyes welled up with tears. I told her how proud her mom would be of her, and I walked away thanking God that the three-week rule is made to be broken.

The three-week rule gives opportunity to grow community, but it should never be an excuse to grow roots that keep us from expanding our hearts.

Our churches are full of people, lots of people—people who need each other, people who try to hide from each other, people who are silently crying out to each other for a little comfort and understanding.

So, my friend, deepen your relationships and you will deepen your heart. Grow community, but don't grow permanent roots. Be willing to move your seat from time to time, and allow your heart to be moved by God as you do.

> *Let us not give up meeting together, as some are in*
> *the habit of doing, but let us encourage one another—*
> *and all the more as you see the Day approaching*
> *(Hebrews 10:25).*

What's Percolating in Me: My Response

Spill the Beans: My Prayer

Thanks a Latte! My Praise

67

One Hundred and One Pizzas

PHIL AND I WERE HEADED OUT THE DOOR for a much-needed date night. The boys and the babysitter took a vote and decided pizza was their dinner choice. Before I left, I made a quick, familiar call to Papa John's.

And until that particular call, I hadn't realized how "familiar" the Rothschild–Papa John's connection had really become!

The call began with the predictable routine, "Thanks for calling Papa John's. Will this be pickup or delivery?" I proceeded to tell the perky female on the other end of the line that it would be delivery and provided her my phone number before she even had a chance to ask for it.

With great excitement, her voice exploded in my earpiece. "Ma'am, this is the hundred and first pizza you've ordered from us! Congratulations."

I was slightly less excited than she was. "Are you sure?" I asked.

She could barely contain her thrill as she scrolled through her computer and recounted when my first purchase was.

"Umm…that's a lot of pizza," I said.

My feeble math brain began to calculate what I must have

spent over the last several years on tomato sauce and mozzarella cheese. "Yikes" I said, "that's a lot of dough—I mean money! Do I get anything free from you for this grand accomplishment?"

She giggled. "Just our congratulations."

After I finished the order, I hung up and got in the van with Phil. I was in shock. Who buys 101 pizzas?

Well, obviously I had, and I was embarrassed. That meant there were 101 times I had not cooked dinner, 101 times I had tossed paper plates on the table instead of setting it, and 101 times I had tipped the delivery guy much too little.

But I refuse to let this pizza milestone be bad news.

There are some positive aspects to this pizzeria connection. It also means that there were 101 occasions over the last several years where our family relaxed a little more, 101 times we lingered at the table a little longer, and 101 times we all agreed about the dinner menu.

If you look at it that way, I have nothing to be embarrassed about. On 101 occasions, I was actually promoting healthy habits in my family. Which really makes pizza the ultimate health food (or not).

So to all of you busy women who keep the pizza industry thriving, I say a hearty congratulations. Don't be ashamed or embarrassed that you're not serving a homemade meal on fine china every night. Instead, celebrate that you're serving your family a memory that makes your home a special place to be.

Find easy ways to keep family life fun.

Believe me, I can think of at least 101.

Taste and see that the LORD is good (Psalm 34:8).

What's Percolating in Me: My Response

_____

_____

_____

_____

Spill the Beans: My Prayer

_____

_____

_____

_____

Thanks a Latte! My Praise

_____

_____

_____

_____

68

Beyond the Stats

DURING A RECENT INTERVIEW, A WRITER asked me about my college experience. "Were there any professors who had a strong influence on you at that transition time in your life?"

The question released a flood of memories. And the strongest of those recollections involved Dr. Ingles, my statistics professor.

During my junior year at Palm Beach Atlantic college, I resigned myself to the sad fact that I would have to take statistics to graduate. Horror stories about the class fellow students called *sadistics* filled me with dread. But my real anxiety was in wondering how I could ever complete a class that required being able to see. I had lost my eyesight only a few years earlier, and I was still learning how to do college (and life) as a blind student.

I remember bemoaning my dilemma to Dr. Ingle in his office. "I must have this class to graduate," I said, "but I just don't know how I can pull it off."

That's when Dr. Ingle surprised me with a dry chuckle. "Maybe *you* can't pull it off, Jennifer," he replied. "But *we* can!"

And so it was, after every class session, Dr. Ingles would take me to his office and painstakingly go through the textbook with me. On test days, he would personally guide me through the exam. Describing formulas and statistical concepts was a meticulous process, but he did so with humor and unwavering endurance.

I actually got an A in the class. I still don't really like statistics, but I will always love Dr. Ingles for teaching me much more than mean, mode, and median. In fact, what he taught me was patience and kindness, and he showed me the lasting lesson that people are worth time and sacrifice. Because he spent the extra time to teach me stats, he made an investment in me and set an extra-high standard for how to treat others and live out my faith.

For you have been called to live in freedom, my brothers and sisters. But don't use your freedom to satisfy your sinful nature. Instead, use your freedom to serve one another in love (Galatians 5:13 NLT).

❧ What's Percolating in Me: My Response

_____

_____

❧ Spill the Beans: My Prayer

_____

_____

❧ Thanks a Latte! My Praise

_____

_____

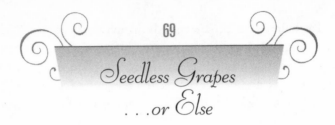

69

Seedless Grapes
. . .or Else

READING THROUGH THE BOOK OF PHILIPPIANS, I stumbled onto the first women's-ministry clash in the New Testament church.

Evidently it was quite a conflict because it merited intervention by the apostle Paul himself. In his letter to the church at Philippi, he wrote, "I implore Euodia and I implore Syntyche to be of the same mind in the Lord" (Philippians 4:2 NKJV).

Paul was asking these two women to settle down and to get along, and in verse 3 he told all the hearers of the letter to help them: "And I urge you also, true companion, help these women who labored with me in the gospel, with Clement also, and the rest of my fellow workers, whose names are in the Book of Life."

Oh yes, the First Community Church of Philippi had a conflict in their women's ministry. Conflicts arise over all sorts of things. Sometimes the differences are about philosophies of ministry; sometimes the tension is simply caused by contrasting personality styles.

Maybe Euodia wanted to serve muffins at the ladies' tea, and Syntyche was convinced that only croissants would do. Maybe Euodia thought it was good stewardship to buy the cheaper grapes from the local market even though they had seeds. But oh no, Syntyche would never serve anything but seedless grapes to the women. Perhaps, Euodia wanted to spend more time in prayer and Syntyche more time in brainstorming. Or maybe they couldn't agree on the purpose of their ministry—was it to bring in or to build up?

No, I haven't sneaked into one of your recent meetings; I just know women. We've not changed much over the centuries. We don't know what the nature of Euodia and Syntyche's disagreement was, but what we do know is that conflict is inevitable.

Conflict can be a result not only of differences but also of selfishness. We may love God and have a common purpose, but that doesn't mean we will have everything in common as we seek to fulfill that purpose. That's why Paul pleaded with these women to "be of the same mind in the Lord."

It can be a reminder to all of us to sacrifice a little of our style and to soften the way we execute our ministry philosophy for the sake of Christ. After all, we don't minister in our own name. The reason we sponsor retreats, lead Bible studies, or shop for seedless grapes is not to glorify our names.

Our conflicts in ministry should never be tools of Satan that cut and divide. Rather, our disagreements should be means of sharpening one another. When we are humble and mature, conflict can become a refining tool of the Holy Spirit to conform us and our ministry to the image of Christ.

As iron sharpens iron,
*   so one man sharpens another*
(Proverbs 27:17).

What's Percolating in Me: My Response

_____

_____

_____

_____

Spill the Beans: My Prayer

_____

_____

_____

_____

Thanks a Latte! My Praise

_____

_____

_____

_____

70

Put Away
Childish Things

LAWANA BLACKWELL WISELY STATED, "Age is no guarantee of maturity."

Now that I'm well into my forties, I understand exactly what she means. My body has certainly grown up as aging has followed its prescribed path. But in some areas of my life, maturity still seems to be catching up.

We don't simply grow chronologically; sometimes we develop unevenly. Our number of years can exceed our degree of emotional, spiritual, or intellectual maturity. Regardless of what our age may be, we can be mature in one realm and still be childish in another. If we don't think about this, we can remain immature as we age.

I have operated under the mistaken notion that childishness and immaturity would just fade away with time. You know, like Paul expressed it in 1 Corinthians 13:11: "When I was a child, I spoke as a child, I understood as a child, I thought as a child; but when I became a man, I put away childish things" (NKJV).

That's all well and good as a principle of life, but the simple fact is that I've ignored some pockets of immaturity in my life.

Why? Well, probably because I assumed that the older I became, the more mature I would become.

The getting older part has all gone according to plan. It's the growing into maturity angle that hasn't always followed suit. And I'm wondering if I'm the only one with a dilemma like this.

When Paul wrote about dealing with childish things in a man or a woman's life, he by no means assured us that the addition of years will assure the subtraction of immaturity. The sad fact is, childish things don't just fade away with time. They must be "put away."

When the season turns to winter, I pull my wool coat from the closet where it has hung since the end of spring. I would have been wearing that heavy coat throughout the entire summer if I had not made a conscious choice to put it away.

My coat doesn't just fade off of my back because the weather warms up, the seasons change, or the time passes. I have to put it away. That's the way we should approach childish things. We need to put them away as well. After they have served their purpose, when the season of adulthood arrives, we need to take special effort to put away childish things.

So, what childish things are still a part of this season of your life?

Reacting impulsively when you don't get your way?

Shouting or pouting when something happens that you don't like?

Living as if you are the center of the universe?

Being unwilling to share your toys—or your time, your forgiveness, or your treasures?

Part of the reason we continue to struggle with childish things far into adulthood is that we have never taken the responsibility for putting them away.

Sydney J. Harris once said, "We have not passed that subtle line between childhood and adulthood until we move from the passive voice to the active voice—that is, until we stop saying, 'It got lost,' and say, 'I lost it.'"

In other words, we must take action to put childishness away and put on maturity.

Just as Paul told the church at Corinth that he "put away" childish things, he told the believers at Rome, Ephesus, and Colosse to be active in "putting on" that which would make them mature in Christ. He admonished them to put on the armor of light, the new self, and love. If we put on these things, they will begin to replace immature thinking, speaking, and reasoning. They will help us replace childish things with maturity.

My friend, I want you clothed in the beautiful garment of love and light, no longer bound by the confining garb of childish things. So determine what you need to put away and what you most need to put on.

Don't just get older—get better!

> *So come on, let's leave the preschool fingerpainting exercises on Christ and get on with the grand work of art. Grow up in Christ…There's so much more. Let's get on with it! (Hebrews 6:1,3 MSG).*

What's Percolating in Me: My Response

_____

_____

_____

_____

Spill the Beans: My Prayer

_____

_____

_____

_____

Thanks a Latte! My Praise

_____

_____

_____

_____

71

Something's Missing

ONE MORNING, PHIL DECIDED TO LABEL the phones in our office. Each of the four of us has a cordless phone, and Phil wanted to make sure they didn't get placed on the wrong desks.

He first took my phone, mentioned it really didn't need a label because it was covered with the remains of my blush, and labeled it anyway with the sticker he made.

He then began to type B-e-c-k-y for the phone of our fabulous correspondence assistant. He placed her sticker on her phone and went back to the computer to finish typing and printing the last two labels.

After he stuck his sticker on his phone, Phil then peeled back and stuck the label for Kathryn, our administrative assistant, on her phone. (Phil and I like to refer to Kathryn as our "indispensable assistant.")

Later that morning as the four of us gathered for staff meeting, Phil proudly directed each of us to our newly labeled phones. Becky confirmed hers was on her desk, and then Kathryn picked hers up and began to read. "Indispensable—ah." She paused at his sweetness and then continued. "Indispensable…aahhh!" she gasped as she tried to read what should have been the abbreviation for *assistant*.

"You forgot the *t!*" Kathryn exclaimed.

"What!" He ran to her phone while Becky and I became engulfed in laughter. "Phil! I can't believe it!" Kathryn protested, trying to appear offended but laughing too hard to make it work. He moaned, apologized, and laughed—and it was the best staff meeting we've ever had!

When labeling something "indispensable asst.," one cannot afford to forget the letter *t*. For one thing, it just neutralizes the compliment you were trying to offer. And more than that, such a missing-in-action letter could lead to embarrassment, hurt feelings—or lawsuits! It's amazing how much importance one little letter can bear.

We are warned in Scripture to note the importance of each letter, each jot and each word of God's Word (Matthew 5:18; Revelation 22:18-19).

The presence or absence of a single letter can totally change a word—in the same way the presence or absence of a word can change the intent of a phrase. For that reason, it's imperative we handle God's Word with respect, precision, and accuracy. (This is one reason why, when I'm doing a Bible study, I like to start with accurate, more literal Bible translations like the New American Standard, the New King James Version, the New International Version, or the English Standard Version.)

I heard a clip on YouTube recently of a very famous woman who had roots in Christianity. She now disavows the claims of the Christian Bible because of what began with the addition of just two words. She recounted hearing her pastor quote, "the Lord thy God is a jealous God."

She was in her late twenties at the time, and this was her response: "Something struck me...I was thinking, 'God is

Omnipresent, and God is also jealous? God is jealous of me?!' Something about that didn't feel right in my spirit, because I believe God is love and that God is in all things. And so, that's when the search for something more than doctrine started to stir within me."

The commencement of her "search" was based on the addition of the words *of me*. Yet the verse that troubled her did not say God was jealous *of her*. The addition of those two little words sent her on a quest that landed her in a place that is far from the doctrine of truth.

The truth of Scripture is offered to us freely from the hand of God, but my heart breaks when it is subject to our misinterpretation. May we all humbly approach His eternal Word with the mindfulness that we are flawed and in need of guidance that only God's Holy Spirit can provide. We need Him to guide us into all truth.

> *This is the one I esteem:*
> *he who is humble and contrite in spirit,*
> *and trembles at my word (Isaiah 66:2).*

What's Percolating in Me: My Response

_____

_____

_____

_____

Spill the Beans: My Prayer

_____

_____

_____

_____

Thanks a Latte! My Praise

_____

_____

_____

_____

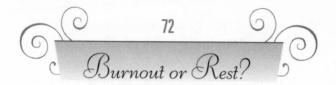
Burnout or Rest?

I'VE TRIED TO LEARN WHAT CAUSES BURNOUT before I smell the smoke! In the past, by the time I detected the burnout, it was like an incinerator, and I was lost in its flames. I'm finally figuring out that rest must be a discipline, and sometimes discipline is hard! (Maybe this is one of those nettlesome maturity issues I wrote about earlier.)

Hebrews 3:19 says, "So we see that they [the children of Israel] were not able to enter [God's rest] because of their unbelief." God has shown me that when I can't rest (or when I'm flat-out unwilling to), I'm actually unwilling to fully trust in Him.

And that, my friend, sounds a lot like unbelief.

My burnout episodes in past days found their roots in the warped, really silly belief that I had to somehow help God accomplish His will. If I didn't strive, I foolishly reasoned, well, the almighty, omnipotent Lord of the universe wouldn't be successful.

Helping God run the universe is a lofty responsibility and a tough business. It can make a girl tired! Obviously, He can handle it Himself just fine. He doesn't need our assistance; He desires our obedience. Jesus tells us, "Take my yoke upon you and learn from me, for I am gentle and humble in heart, and you will find rest for your souls" (Matthew 11:29).

I remember reading something Chuck Swindoll wrote years

ago that went like this: "The zealot declares, 'I'd rather *burn* out than *rust* out.' But really, what's the difference? Either way you're out!"

I can't really think of a place in Scripture where God calls us to burn ourselves to a crisp in His service. In fact, He calls us to rest. He calls us to discipline our souls to find rest in Him, not in our accomplishments on His behalf.

Would you drive your car if the gas tank were empty? Of course not. But how often do you keep on driving yourself even when *you* are empty? Benjamin Franklin once said, "He that can take rest is greater than he that can take cities."

Do you know why he compares the ability to rest with world domination? Because both require discipline. We must discipline ourselves to rest—emotionally, mentally, and physically. (And remember, Jennifer is preaching to herself here!)

To really rest means we submit our control to God's calendar, surrender our plans to His direction, and yield our time to His schedule. Even God made time in His busy creation project to rest! So for you to do the same is to follow His example. Disciplining yourself to rest is an act of good stewardship.

The discipline of rest brings freedom that doesn't exist in the ashes of burnout. When we allow ourselves to burn out, we are rendered ineffective to all the goals and tasks that were once our priorities. To discipline ourselves to rest now is far easier than to dig ourselves out of a fire pit later.

God commanded the ancient Israelites to observe the Sabbath every seven days. And He even instructed them to give their land a rest every seven years. My friend, if the dirt needs a rest so it can continue to be fruitful, so do you!

He said to them, "Come with me by yourselves to a quiet place and get some rest" (Mark 6:31).

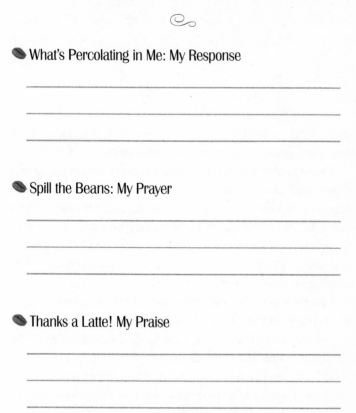

🫘 What's Percolating in Me: My Response

_____

_____

_____

🫘 Spill the Beans: My Prayer

_____

_____

_____

🫘 Thanks a Latte! My Praise

_____

_____

_____

73

The Melody
of Silence

DO YOU EVER FIND YOURSELF QUESTIONING why you couldn't keep from saying something you know you shouldn't have said?

I seem to be constantly saying things I later regret, wishing with all my heart that I hadn't opened my mouth. But it's no surprise that my words spill out with such fervency and frequency—my thoughts are constantly chattering inside my brain demanding an audience!

I wonder why I still deal with this after all these years. (Another maturity issue...sigh.)

I guess what forced these thoughts to the surface once again was being with my dad this past week. He has always seemed *so* disciplined in what he says, what he doesn't say, and when he chooses to speak or remain silent.

If I ask him about it now, I know he'll reply that it's because he's hard of hearing. But I'm not buying any of that. He's had this mastery as long as I can remember. Time and again through the years I have watched his restraint, listened to his speech, heard his silence, and thought, *I must learn silence.*

Have you ever thought about silence as something we can learn?

When I think of silence, I don't think of its importance the way my fellow Missourian Mark Twain once jabbed: "It is better to keep your mouth closed and let people think you are a fool than to open it and remove all doubt." Though there is merit to Mr. Twain's advice, I'm referring to a deeper silence. The kind of silence that manifests itself in well-ordered thought, careful speech, and the willingness to simply hold the tongue.

Mother Teresa said, "We need to find God, and he cannot be found in noise and restlessness. God is the friend of silence. See how nature—trees, flowers, grass—grows in silence; see the stars, the moon and the sun, how they move in silence…We need silence to be able to touch souls."

I believe if we are to experience the discipline of silence in our thoughts and speech, we must surround ourselves with silence from time to time. To simply be still, to allow a soul silence to settle over us, invites God.

Silence invites contemplation and confession.

Silence allows for revelation and responsiveness to God.

Silence ushers out the noise of life and makes room for God's presence to overwhelm us.

Silence lets you hear God's voice more clearly. When we allow our surroundings to be hushed from time to time, we become enveloped by the wordless wonder of who God is and who He created us to be.

The inner strength and Spirit-control that show up in our silence also show up as we share with others. If we begin to learn silence, others will eventually appreciate and learn from its fruit in our lives.

Learning to be still influences the way we think. Our thought patterns influence what we say and, equally as important, what we don't say.

In relationships with others, silence invites response; it defers and initiates rather than crowds and inhibits.

Honestly, sometimes I have regretted speaking, and other times I have regretted my silence. But the ratio between those two regrets is probably ten to one!

With quieter inner and outer surroundings, we hear the music that plays only in silence, and it engages us to hum along with its haunting melody of restraint.

Marcel Marceau, the world-famous French mime artist who created Bip, the white-faced clown, once said; "Music and silence combine strongly because music is done with silence, and silence is full of music."

Shhh...can you hear it?

In repentance and rest is your salvation,
in quietness and trust is your strength
(Isaiah 30:15).

What's Percolating in Me: My Response

_____

_____

Spill the Beans: My Prayer

_____

_____

Thanks a Latte! My Praise

_____

_____

74

A Prayer for All Seasons

> Let the words of my mouth and
>   the meditation of my heart
> Be acceptable in Your sight,
> O LORD, my strength and my
>   Redeemer (Psalm 19:14 NKJV).

HOW I LOVE THAT VERSE!

It's one of my favorites, not only because I can still hear my grandmother quote it but also because I pray it all the time, and I have for years. The verse is so incredibly practical because it gives both the *standard* for our talk (acceptable in Your sight) and the *source* for our talk (my strength and Redeemer).

Our standard for the words we speak both out loud and to ourselves is not merely what is acceptable to us, but rather what is acceptable to God. In our own sight, our self talk may appear fine. But imagine the God of the universe, or Jesus, His Son, sitting in your living room and listening to you talk to yourself. Imagine Him in the passenger seat as you drive alone and talk to yourself. Imagine Him in your bathroom as you look in the mirror and say the same old destructive things to yourself.

Simply put, imagine that He is standing at the door of your thought closet, hearing each phrase of self talk that comes in. Imagine that everything you say to yourself is spoken in His sight. Would you still say the same things to yourself? Would you speak in the same way to yourself if you knew He was listening?

By the way, God *does* listen to your words and your thoughts. Every one them.

Psalm 94:9 asks: "Does he who implanted the ear not hear?" And the psalmist confirms, "Evening, morning and noon...he hears my voice" (55:17).

He hears what no one else does. And He cares about what you say to yourself because He cares about *you*. He is your Father, the one who made you. To insult yourself is to insult Him. If you knew for certain that He was standing beside you through the hours of your day (and He is), you would most likely hold your thoughts captive at the door of your thought closet! I would never call myself an insulting name if I could see God standing right next to me, gazing attentively. I can just imagine Him saying, "Oh, Jennifer...What did you say? That's not right. I don't make idiots. Jesus died so you would know who you are and live like it. My daughter, you are not an idiot."

Seeing God in the middle of our thought closets gives us a standard to meet with our own soul talk. But in our weakness, we often need a little help choosing and controlling our soul talk. God is not only the standard of our healthy soul talk; He can also be the source of it.

The psalmist called God his strength and his Redeemer. In other words, God was the source from whom the psalmist could draw wise words and thoughts. God's strength is our source when we are weak.

To keep vigilant control over our thoughts is difficult, isn't it? We are weak, and we need strength. My grandmother used to say (and perhaps yours did too), "If you can't say something nice, don't say anything at all!" That was usually referring to me ranting about someone or something I didn't like. But her grandmotherly admonishment applies wisely to our soul talk.

God can strengthen us to keep a guard over our lips. If we can't say anything wise, productive, or edifying, God can strengthen us to say nothing at all! When you feel weak, draw from the source—His strength.

Let me challenge you to memorize Psalm 19:14 if you haven't already. Meditate on it during the day. It will become like wallpaper in your thought closet! It will constantly keep the standard and source of wise soul talk in the front of your mind.

I leave you with a little conversation between the Lord and the prophet Jeremiah, whose belittling self talk had convinced him that he was too inexperienced, ineffective, and immature to be of any use to God. But the Lord took issue with those negative, self-defeating words of the prophet.

And the rest is history!

The word of the LORD came to him...

"Before I formed you in the womb I knew you,
before you were born I set you apart;
I appointed you as a prophet to the nations."

*"Ah, Sovereign LORD," I said, "I do not know
how to speak; I am only a child."*

*But the LORD said to me, "Do not say, 'I am
only a child.' You must go to everyone I send you
to and say whatever I command you. Do not be
afraid of them, for I am with you and will rescue
you," declares the LORD (Jeremiah 1:2,5-8).*

🌿

What's Percolating in Me: My Response

_____

_____

Spill the Beans: My Prayer

_____

_____

Thanks a Latte! My Praise

_____

_____

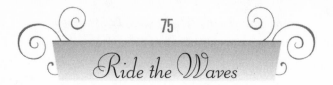

75

Ride the Waves

IN EARLY 1992, SOME REMARKABLE PASSENGERS went overboard during a fierce storm in the North Pacific. Nearly 30,000 Chinese-made plastic bath toys began to spread out across the sea, slowly making their way over the waves.

For 16-plus years now, yellow ducks, green frogs, blue turtles, and red beavers have created quite a colorful flotilla! Their journey has taken them far and wide across the oceans of our planet.

In the Arctic Ocean, a number of them were frozen as décor in bright oversized ice cubes. After floating through the Arctic Ocean, some of them bobbed and dipped their way along the entire length of Greenland, and some have even drifted down the eastern seaboard of the United States.

According to Fox News, the seafaring tub toys began life in a Chinese factory and were being shipped to the United States when three 40-foot containers were washed overboard. Two-thirds of the castaways drifted south through the tropics, landing months later on the shores of Indonesia, Australia, and South America.

Another 10,000 of the toys floated north, and by the end of the year were off the coast of Alaska and heading back westward. On their journey, many of the little fellas were stranded in circulating currents, many more were blown ashore, and some unfortunates were actually crushed by icebergs.

It's tough being a plucky little ducky on a big ocean!

Oceanographers predicted that some would spend years trapped in the arctic ice, moving at the rate of only one mile a day, and eventually land on the shores of Great Britain.

By the time many of these survivors make landfall—somewhere!—they will be ragged, torn, deteriorated, and bleached white by the sun and salt.

I think it would be fun to find one (probably not too likely in Missouri). Sure, they would be weathered and worn, and maybe nobody would really want to bathe with one, but each of those little toys is what I want to be…an overcomer!

You and I don't really know where the current of God's plan will take us, do we? We may end up far, far from the shores where we imagined we would spend our lives. Like those waterlogged little warriors, we may find ourselves just trying to keep our heads above water when life's storms begin to roll. Sometimes our journey feels long, goes slowly, and lands us in foreign places.

Those plastic bath toys overcame insurmountable odds, and by the time you and I arrive at heaven's shore, we will have faced our share of turbulence too. So, what does it mean to overcome?

The Greek translation for the word *overcome* in 1 John 5:4 is *nikao*, which means to come off victorious.

To describe Christ followers as overcomers is not to say they win every battle in life. It is rather saying that no matter what—even in death—they will hold fast to their faith. An overcomer endures temptations and perseveres through trials and persecutions.

The ones who ride the waves of this life, holding firm to their faith, are those who are unwilling to quit. Overcomers persevere regardless of what the journey is like.

They are described in the book of Revelation this way:

> They overcame him
> by the blood of the Lamb
> and by the word of their testimony;
> for they did not love their lives so much
> as to shrink from death (Revelation 12:11).

My friend, someday we too will finally arrive on a distant shore, and what matters is not how difficult the journey, but how beautiful the shore. Our victory isn't in eliminating the adversity, our victory is in faithfully finishing the journey. For those who overcome, a crown of life is promised. So if you feel as if you're going under, being tossed about, or just trying to keep your head above water...ride the waves, my friend. The tumult of your travels here cannot compare with the triumph of your arrival in heaven someday. You will trade in your weary, worn, weathered sojourning suit for a glittering crown.

Blessed is the man who perseveres under trial,
because when he has stood the test, he will receive the
crown of life that God has promised to those who love
him (James 1:12).

What's Percolating in Me: My Response

_____

_____

_____

_____

Spill the Beans: My Prayer

_____

_____

_____

_____

Thanks a Latte! My Praise

_____

_____

_____

_____

Conclusion

YES, IT'S TRUE. I FREELY ADMIT IT. One of my best-loved activities in all of life is savoring an excellent cup of coffee with a couple of friends in the warm, fragrant confines of a good coffee shop.

There's something about being surrounded by the laughter, the conversations, the sometimes strange music, and the fragrance of delicate little pastries and newly roasted java that makes me warm all over. (A piece of fresh, moist pumpkin bread doesn't do any harm to that mental image!) I don't even mind the conversation-challenging noise of the grinding machine because I know what it's producing back there behind the counter!

That's the flavor I've wanted to capture in this little book.

There are so many women I've met around the country at conferences and events that I would love to spend a little more time with so I could hear their stories, laugh at the crazy things that have happened in our lives, shed a few tears over their heartaches and longings…and of course join them for something rich, smooth, and caffeinated!

Mostly I'd like to tell as many women as I can how the Lord can bring light, hope, wisdom, perspective, and even joy into the darkest and seemingly most hopeless valleys and dead-end roads of life.

Coffee is wonderful, lattes are worthy beverages, and caramel macchiatos make me rejoice that God invented taste buds, but it really isn't about the coffee. Followers of Jesus Christ were encouraging one another and enjoying fellowship with their Lord and with each other for at least a thousand years before the first Ethiopian goat herder crouching by his highland fire tasted his first sip of the first bitter brew. (And probably said, "Pass the cream, please.")

All over the world, coffee or no coffee, women have found that a living connection to Jesus Christ has given them the inspiration, the perseverance, the renewed vision, and the emotional and spiritual strength to face any circumstance that life throws at them.

I've had to deal with blindness in my life, and God willing, you will never have to walk that particular pathway. But you have your own set of issues, your own difficult and treacherous stretches of life's highway I may never have to face. (If we ever bump into each other in a Starbucks, we can tell each other all about it.)

But when it's all said and done....

The lift isn't in the coffee, it's in the Lord. The richness isn't in the espresso, it's in relationship with God's Son. The strength, boldness, and uncompromising flavor in life doesn't come from carefully roasted beans, but from God's indwelling Holy Spirit, whom God has promised will be our never-failing Counselor, Companion, Guide, Teacher, and Friend.

God (who in His wisdom created coffee) wants to be our all in all. He wants to be the answer to the deep-down cries of our spirit. He stands ready to become our never-failing source of inner strength, allowing us to grow into the kind of sisters, daughters, wives, and mothers we really want to be in our heart of hearts—but can never quite become on our own.

Take a coffee break with *Him* today. Open His timeless Word and wrap yourself in the warmth of His counsel and the fragrance of His presence.

He'll be there. When you're ready, He's ready.

Let's keep the conversation going. . .

Thanks for spending some coffee breaks with me!

I don't know you by name, but I would love to. It would mean so much to keep in touch, to hear your story, and to hear how you keep your faith fresh and grounded. If you visit my website below, we can stay connected through my blog and through my email newsletter called Java with Jennifer.

Also, I would love to meet you at one of my Fresh Grounded Faith conferences, where we have such a good time laughing, learning, and growing in our faith. Visit FreshGroundedFaith.com to find out when and where we can share a cup of Fresh Grounded Faith with thousands of new friends.

> Thanks a latte my friend,
> Jennifer

Visit www.JenniferRothschild.com
or www.FreshGroundedFaith.com

or write to

Jennifer Rothschild
4319 S. National Avenue, Suite 303
Springfield, MO 65810

Other Great Resources from
Jennifer Rothschild

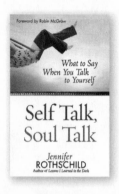

SELF TALK, SOUL TALK: WHAT TO SAY WHEN YOU TALK TO YOURSELF
Featured on ABC's *Good Morning America*, Jennifer's message in this book is important for every woman: Words are powerful—especially the words you speak to yourself. Jennifer shares practically and helpfully from her own life and from Scripture to show how you can turn your words—and your life—around for good.

ISBN 978-0-7369-2072-8

ME, MYSELF AND LIES: A THOUGHT CLOSET MAKEOVER
Based on *Self Talk, Soul Talk*, this new individual and small group book and DVD Bible study provides practical strategies to help you "clean out your thought closet" and become a woman who lives by the truth. It features six weeks of interactive material for daily personal study. The Leader Kit includes seven teaching lessons by Jennifer on DVD.

ISBN 978-1-4158-6644-3 Member Book
UPC 634337016276 Leader Kit with DVDs

LESSONS I LEARNED IN THE DARK: STEPS TO WALKING BY FAITH, NOT BY SIGHT

This bestselling book was featured on *Dr. Phil, Good Morning America,* and *The Billy Graham Television Special.* With warmth and humor, Jennifer shows you how to walk by faith, and not by sight. Beth Moore says, "*Lessons I Learned in the Dark* is gripping. I don't know the person to whom it has nothing to say."

ISBN 1-59052-047-5 Trade Paperback
ISBN 978-1-4243-4179-5 Audio Book

WALKING BY FAITH BIBLE STUDY

This bestselling study is based on *Lessons I Learned in the Dark.* The member book features six weeks of interactive material for daily personal study and includes a leader guide. The leader kit includes seven teaching segments and is also available on DVD. A *Walking by Faith* music CD also available.

ISBN 0-6330-9932-5 Member Book
ISBN 0-6330-9145-6 Leader Kit
UPC 8-09812-00502-5 Music CD

FINGERPRINTS OF GOD BIBLE STUDY

Based on Jennifer's book of the same name, the member book features six weeks of interactive material for daily personal study. A leader kit with seven teaching segments is also available on DVD.

ISBN 1-4158-2088-0 Member Book
ISBN 1-4158-2090-2 Leader Kit
ISBN 1-59052-530-2 Hardcover Trade Book